VIEWS *from the* FEN

CAMBRIDGE PUBLISHING GROUP

First published in Great Britain in 1994 by
Cambridge Publishing Group, 20 Perowne Street,
Cambridge CB1 2AY.

Typesetting and production: Town Crier, Cambridge

Cover photograph: Peter Dunne

Printed by University Printing Services, Cambridge

A catalogue record for this book is available from The British Library.

ISBN 0 9520482 1 3

Contents

The Village

A LAUGHING GIRL....A DARK YOUNG MAN

What with that lovely Indian summer having come to a squelching halt with chill winter hard on its heels methinks it might be a good moment to warm the old cockles with a touch of romance, and a large lump of that particular commodity came rumbling into our village at the weekend.

It came in the form of an old caravan, of which more later. But first, try if you can to imagine how things were in one particular village out in the fens just after the end of the first world war for that is when our tale begins. It would have been a harsh world untouched by modernity, gripped by poverty, the community bound by a stern sense of religious propriety.

Pleasure had to be homemade, travel, apart from occasional trips to market, non-existent. Imagine also, therefore, the thoughts of a young and pretty girl living out there, anxious for romance, fun and adventure. Then, hey presto... suddenly, out of the black fen comes a gaudy procession. Painted caravans, horse-drawn vehicles piled high with all the fun of the fair. The stalls are set out, there is music and giddying swings and the village erupts into rare festivity.

There is also a handsome young traveller working one of the stalls and before the fair is ended he and the pretty young girl are in love. In those days an impossible situation, a union not to be countenanced by village society. Falling in love with a fairground boy was the stuff of penny dreadfuls. It didn't happen in real life. It couldn't work.

But it did at that distant fair out in the fens. And when the fair moved off on its travels it took with it the dark young man and the girl who was to become his bride. And the connection with the caravan which arrived in our village on Saturday? Why, that was the very caravan which the parents of the young traveller had made for him and his bride as a wedding present. They went away in it on their honeymoon, the van all cosy with its double bed, its little fireplace, its sturdy frame. I know not where they wandered in it together over the years but I like to believe they were happy travellers, the laughing girl and the dark young man.

It's not a traditional gypsy-style caravan, but a lantern-topped showman's van, hand-built with an air of reliability about it and it has been bought by my friend Dick Bourne who plans to restore it as he has so many other fine but neglected vintage vehicles. It stands in his father's field at the end of our village street and merely to catch a glimpse of it is to return to a slower, gentler age. Dick, who found it in Ramsey, understands that the lass who eloped all those years ago may still be alive. If she is what tales she must have to tell. What memories of another world. I'd give my old shut-knife and half a crown for the chance of a chat with her.

GARLICKY FOREIGNERS BEWARE

Now when Caesar first first plodded into Gaul he made no scruple to profess that "he had rather be first in a village than second in Rome" and that goes for me and a lot of other sensible folk for many of us recognised long ago that of all units of habitation the village is the most agreeable. (Actually, that's not quite what Caesar was getting at but it's of little importance since he is in no position to argue with me).

And if you are beginning to wonder why I discourse thus about the village in this mind-freezing weather it is because I read with horror this week of a campaign which is soon to be launched "to arrest and reverse the economic and social decline of Europe's villages".

A conference is to be held (naturally) in Germany in March and a new body has been set up (naturally) which calls itself (deep breath here): the Council for the Conservation and Reanimation of Europe's Villages and Small Towns and a more dangerous-sounding outfit I have yet to discover.

The geezer behind this caper is Francis Noel-Baker, former Labour MP for Swindon (a charming, unspoiled little hamlet) who no doubt needs some excuse to keep himself flitting about in luxury now that he no longer clutters up the Whitehall corridors of power. But can you imagine it? A bunch of European do-gooders reanimating us? Well, let me tell the new Council for whatever-it-is that if they come poking their Froggy and Hun Noses into our affairs in Swaffham Bulbeck they're in for a startling surprise to say nothing of an uphill struggle because they couldn't reanimate us lot not even if they bunged the entire cast of the Folies Bergere into the cricket pavilion with free champers thrown in.

You see, before they have even begun their task of folly, they have misunderstood the very purpose of the village, particularly the English variety.

Animation is the absolute opposite to our desired way of life. It summons up dreadful and disturbing visions of excitement, galvanism, agitation, liveliness, high spirits and exhilaration. But that sort of tiring nonsense is for the frisky townies and not for us slow and bucolic peasants.

We can manage to get animated in our own way thank you very much and without any help from outside. We take our time over it and I confess that the last occasion it happened to me was when I grew a radish of such succulent magnitude that even Percy Blinco had to catch his breath in admiration.

Nope, there are folks hereabouts who have no wish to become animated and, indeed, are only likely to become animated at the first appearance in the village of a group of garlicky foreigners intent upon waking us from our glorious lethargy, our snoring contentments, our splendid decline.

Some chap whose name escapes me summed the whole thing up rather nicely when he said: "If you would be known, and not know, vegetate in a village; if you would know, and be not known , live in a city". Perzackly. So shove off Noel-Baker and leave us alone.

BOB THOMSON'S STROLL

Standing outside the village stores the other sweltering morn, torn by indecision as to whether to have one in the Black 'Oss or The Oak I espied the stolid figure of one of our community who has this week returned from a long working stint out in Hong Kong wherever that may be. I watched him walking slowly across the recreation ground, over the shaven surface of the cricket square and on under young conker trees before turning with languid stride to march over the mown meadow, through the kissing gate on his way for lunch in his lovely cottage. It was all immensely still, birds drooping on the perch, barely a sound. I wondered: is he missing the skyscrapers of Kowloon; is he thinking of the sun coming up like thunder out of China 'cross the bay? Or, like me, is Bob Thomson thinking of the effortless joys of English life?

BILL'S SMITHY

Among the vital ingredients for the making of a true English village I would list a cricket pitch for fun, a pub for escape, a church for brides, a rich lord for tapping and a smithy for sheer, glorious, unashamed nostalgic joy. At least one village in these parts could claim to satisfy each of those requirements until last week when, after 64 years of service to the community, it lost its blacksmith's shop. I make no apology for chronicling its passing for we shall not see its like again. The end came when the smith himself, Bill Sargent, a toweringly youthful 84, died suddenly with no thought of retirement on his mind and was deeply mourned by many of differing classes, ages and persuasions. And on Saturday morning the main street of Lode whose thatched cottages slumber in the lee of Anglesey Abbey, was filled by those who had come to see the tools of old Bill's craft sold. I went not to buy but to remember and there were others like me who stood silent as the auctioneer called out the magic names of everyday artefacts of a vanishing world..... anvils, bellows, thatching pins, a grindstone, unpointed harrow tines, shoeing nails and, of course, horse shoes. But a village smithy is not merely the sum of its contents nor the value of a length of flat, unworked iron. Bill Sargent worked in that shed since he was a lad of 20 after learning his craft in Teversham - he was shoeing horses before the Kaiser got uppety and ended real civilisation - and his smithy was much, much more. It was the living link between an England of nuclear power and that England of trundling haywains, of untravelled villagers, an England which just sometimes clings to the cliff-edge of memory through the lives of men like Bill Sargent.

Bill's smithy was something else, too. Of a morning, any morning, inside the dark interior lit by fierce flames on the iron-bound forge and sun chinking in through loose, red pantiles on the crumbly roof, old men would stand and talk and while Bill worked on with infinite care, stories of past deeds would be interrupted by the ringing clang of hammer on anvil. And of an afternoon, any afternoon, there would be children in and around the smithy, listening and watching and sniffing the curious, steamy smell of red-hot iron dipped into cooling water. When Bill began work in that old shed on the corner opposite, of course, the Three Horseshoes, ancients were talking around his forge of their youth before the old Queen's time. There were men there who talked of Waterloo as casually as some talk today of the Somme. That's what Bill's smithy was. A history book.

MOULDY

Upon the vigil of All Hallows there was much screeching and joyful wailing about the village as masked and white-shrouded kids skittered about the streets with their Hallowe'en lanterns planning their campaign of "trick or treat". Unaware that I was earwigging on the other side of our garden wall they discussed the treasures they had plundered from local households last year - money from this house, chocolates from that, bags of sweets from another. "What about the Jeacocks?", enquired one tiny voice. "Don't bother with them", came the instant reply. "They only give you mouldy old biscuits".

WELL, WHY NOT?

Villages should be fun, slightly crazy perhaps, eccentric certainly and every now and again they should go off the rails in a wanton fantasy of sheer joyful exuberance. For if there is a more pleasing form of community in which to exist than the English village (give or take a few exceptions like the Cheltenham Ladies' College and the Fellowship of Trinity College) then I'm the filling in a bar of Turkish delight. And if you find it difficult to believe me then book yourself into a high rise apartment block in the grimy metropolis for a week and then call me a liar. Thus, if for no other reason than to celebrate one's luck at living in a village, it seems not only reasonable but obligatory to go bananas occasionally which is precisely what we are going to do in our parish come the heady days of June and for eight days we intend to let ourselves go. We will leave behind our normal constraints with the same delight as a stout lady discarding her corsets. All the village organisations will contribute to the general jollity from schoolkids to the over 60s; the streets will be awash with bunting, our gardens will be given an extra polish in case of visitors, there'll be Gilbert and Sullivan in one of the big barns, a dance in another, a family service in our lovely church, a flower festival, bygones exhibition, a 'funny' cricket match (nothing unusual there, come to think of it). I dare say there will be some beer drunk and a kiss or two snatched among the fritillary behind the sports pavilion. Money will be made, of course, and profits will help the church and local organisations but that's not the real point of it at all. People hereabouts suddenly determined to enjoy themselves for the very simple reason that they love living here and the realisation came upon them that the time was ripe for an emotional, reasonless beano. I mention all this to one end: why don't you have a go yourselves? If not this year then maybe next. And if you are a townie, organise a knees-up in the street one fine summer's day.

TRAP-BALL AND MARBLES

Every year as spring approaches I grieve for the passing of the many glories which we old 'uns took for granted in the fragant countryside of our youth - the golden carpets of cowslips, the fairy forests of harebells, ponds and troughs stuffed with frog spawn and newts, traffic-free roads filled with the shouts of children playing the old games of bat and trap, battledore and shuttlecok, hoop bowling, hopscotch and, of course marbles. Wild flowers have fallen to herbicides, the poor frog to pesticides, the lovely games to the dread computer and video. But hope's perpetual breath breathes on and I believe that one of the blessings which will come with the imminent revolution in the farming industry will be an inevitable return to simpler ways in the countryside. There will be reduced requirements for the ubiquitous plough and for intensive grazing and ancient grasslands will re-appear with, I pray, their attendant wild flowers. Will the old games come back also? I fear not. Which is a huge pity for they linked us to the very thread of history. For instance, trap-ball can be traced back to the beginning of the fourteenth century, marbles have been substitutes for bowls for centuries and the whipping of tops was known in the days of Virgil. Alas, the wizardry of electronics has vanquished the charm of tradition and I believe our children are the poorer for it.

CRICKET'S HUGE EXCITEMENT

I slipped home from the violent streets on Saturday to the peace of the cricket match being played on our lovingly tended recreation ground in the village. At one stage of the game there were three supporters watching the proceedings, Percy Blinco, George Ambrose and me with between us about 200 years experience of sitting back in the sun and criticising the players. A distant plume of smoke signalled a burning stubble field - or had the nasty natives of Newmarket risen again? - but otherwise there was nothing to disturb our somnolence other than the loveliest of all sounds, the smack of leather on willow. The game slowed down and Percy nudged me into sudden wakefulness. He said: "Tell you what, bor, if these old boys don't increase their scoring rate the crowd will start drifting off".

GOLDEN CANDLE-GLOW

Astonishing thing happened on the way home from the Oak the other evening. That rather splendid thunderstorm and its attendant and most beneficial cloudburst led, as is usual on such occasions in this remote part of Europe, to the electricity going off. And that meant, of course, that the tellies all dimmed and folk were left wringing hands in frustration and wondering how on earth a few minutes could be spent without the soporific aid of the idiot box in the corner. But, lo, suddenly, the village street finds people standing at garden gates actually talking to each other. Here and there a room is lit by golden candle-glow with children playing table games. On the evening air cooled by the rain floats nature's incense, the rich odour of cascading honeysuckle. Then the flaming lights flash on again and figures drift back to catch up with a half-missed murder film and guttering candles are outshone by the harshness of the overhead bulb. Still, it was an exquisite change while it lasted.

HAPPY, HAPPY MOKE

Nothing if not exciting, this life of ours out in the country. Take Sunday morning. Considerable to-do in the Abbey field at the end of the village whence has escaped Mrs Bourne's pet donkey, a placid creature given to making strange noises and giving much pleasure to local children, although it always displays less than friendly attitudes to my wife, thus showing some finesse in its breeding. The vanished moke left behind two large clues in the road which suggested it had turned right and was therefore heading towards the other Abbey in the neighbourhood, Anglesey Abbey. Consternation! Would Lord Fairhaven glance up from his breakfast black-pudding to find a strange donkey nibbling his cabbage patch? After a night away from home, Sam the donkey was found in contented mood in a meadow down by the Lode. How had he spent his night of freedom? Perhaps we shall never know. But I tell you this: there was a very satisfied look about the old chap. Hope he enjoyed himself.

GOOD LAD!

Winter is a-drawing-on and the proof lies in the sounds of the country: the thud of seven-pound axes cleaving logs, the scream of chain-saws biting through thick timber. We have piles of elm and beech in the woodyard at the end of the house all ready to be split. It is my pleasure to take the axe to the straight-grained beech through which it passes as a hot needle through butter. I leave the near-impossible twisted toughness of the elm to Simon and that, I reckon, is just about the right way to organise a father-son relationship.

COME - SPLIT A LOG

Popped round to the wood yard the other cold and damp morning armed with the seven pound axe I bought for my missus' birthday some years ago intent on splitting a few logs when a sad thought suddenly assailed me. Well, to be accurate, it sort of drifted over me for my brain, like the rest of my body, is built more for ambling than dashing. But the thought did finally arrive and it was this: what with central heating, there are millions of folk these days who will never experience the sheer joy of a simple activity like splitting a log. There are, you say, probably more important matters to be discussed but the fact is that a pleasurable life is one which is lived a bit at a time and in which small happinesses are self-produced. Like log-splitting.

This solitary task has a multiplicity of varying elements attached to it. There is the requirement of skill for to be able to swing the big axe accurately is not an instantly acquired talent. Get the balance and the swing wrong and you are certain to do yourself an unmentionable mischief. But get them right and there is the exquisite pleasure of perfect timing to be compared only with the hitting of a six with a straight drive over the bowler's head or the ordering of a pint a second before the landlord calls time. There is the knowledge that, unless the old heart is a bit dicky, you are doing yourself a power of physical good for there can be few exercises which involve the use of so many different muscles at the same time. There is the further knowledge that a secondary pleasure will shortly be yours for it is a sad soul which cannot appreciate the charm of a log fire. The time taken by the splitting of the logs can be used for the peaceful contemplation of the glass of port you will allow yourself whilst sitting beside the crackling fruits of your endeavours. Or it can be utilised for the plotting of the downfall of ancient enemies. Furthermore, if you've just had a nasty letter from the bank manager you can, within the wink of an eye, convert the log standing before you into his head and derive huge fun from chopping it exactly down the middle.

So all in all it's a joyous pastime. And now another thought comes meandering into the old cranium. Why should I be so selfish as to keep the pleasures of log-splitting all to myself? Why don't I share them with the less fortunate? Please feel free to pop round and slice through a few hundred logs for me. I promise not to charge too much for the privilege.

GINGER CAKE AND BROWN ALE

This year the missus and I agreed that we would not join in the bonfire night celebrations since the children are temporarily grown out of that particular excitement. But then, as the blaze across the road in the Bournes' field lit up their ancient house and the walnut trees stood out like bronzes against the black sky we couldn't resist it and in a trice were wellied and strolling over to the Abbey. Later, in their 12th century undercroft built of clunch by men born 500 years before Guy Fawkes, we watched a new generation of toddlers whooping it up. We washed ginger cake down with brown ale and as the fire sank and the trees were swallowed by the devouring dark we meandered back home. I do hope we never grow up.

SNOWY SHANGRI-LA

Call me an incurable old romantic if you like but the plain fact is I am exceedingly fond of the stuff. Snow, that is. Not that grey, mushy rubbish you townies slop about in but the variety we have out here in the country, white as a princess's bridal gown, clean as an archbishop's joke. And after Sunday night's tempest we woke in this village to find to our astonishment that so much of it had been blown onto the roads that we were completely cut off and so, for a few delicious hours we knew the delights of mythical Shangri La, trapped in our own tiny paradise.

Nobody, not even Percy Blinco who sailed in with the Ark, could remember the village being marooned but as news of our total isolation swept through the parish the most remarkable thing happened. Whole families poured out of their white-sprayed homes, kids whooping, women laughing and men grinning sheepishly at the sudden realisation that nature, with one gigantic gesture overnight, had removed from them the necessity to make decisions about their work and had salved their consciences by imposing upon them a day's truancy.

We couldn't get out - and they couldn't get in to us. No mail, so no final demands; no papers, so no bad news and, joy of all joys, the phones even went on the blimp so it was nearly impossible to speak to the clots still toiling in the outside world. From the lump which we call a hill at the back of the village the scene was straight out of a Dutch painting, the streets dotted with groups black against the stark white background, dogs dashing, children slithering and sledging, and for perhaps the first and last time in our lives the community was a whole, an entity. And such goodwill everywhere. Feuding neighbours helped to dig each other out, there was much back-slapping as families meandered around the village oohing at this drift and aahing at another. Here again the British were united in the face of adversity and there was an air of cold carnival about the place.

I met only one curmudgeon who fretted for the sanctuary of his dreary office, but then he wouldn't enjoy himself if he was thrown into a vat of champagne with a line of chorus girls. Elsewhere everyone frolicked and the Oak and the Black 'Oss were packed as stories of the previous night's terrors grew taller. They swore that George Weir drank so much scotch to fight off the freezing vapours that his breath melted seven-foot drifts down in Longmeadow.

I don't know about that but I was there in the Oak when, after lunch, some clot announced the road to Quy was open. In the horrified silence a voice slurred with contentment said: "Well, go and close it again."

THE PREROGATIVE OF BRAVE YOUTH

The other morning I strolled up the village street, cut across Butler's Meadow, sauntered along the edge of the cricket field. Morning mist still hung on the cobwebs, apples hung over the meadow wall and conkers hung high on the chestnut trees.

Mrs Debenham sailed past on her bike, laughing and shouting a greeting, old Mrs Marsh stopped to tell me with pride of the achievements of her grandchildren and Ted Fletcher paused to inform me that his missus and our old friend, Ann, was in good working order.

We had a laugh or several in the Post Office and I walked back through the warming morning whence I had come and sat me down to write an exhultation, a paean of praise to the English village, especially our very own.

I wrote of the village's sense of gentleness, of its serenity, of all the small joys which, when amalgamated, burgeon into that greatest glory of the English village - an overwhelming sense of truly belonging. I wrote of jolly happenings, funny tales, merry anecdotes. I was filled with a soothing content; I had no sense of foreboding, no inkling of disaster.

And then the gentle Mrs Perrett phoned me from her home in the High Street in our village. Many of you will know her and her husband Ron for they have been proprietors for years of Almond's wet fish shop in Newmarket Road, Cambridge.

Mrs Perrett told me quietly that their son James had died in the snows of the Alps and his inseparable pal Dave Howie, whose father is a Cambridge professor, was missing, presumed dead also.

Both young men were aged 21. Dave was head boy at the Perse School in Cambridge and James was senior prefect. They played rugby together, they Scouted together, they climbed together. They both won places at Cambridge University, James at Jesus College, Dave at St John's College. Dave had still to take his important exams but James had been awarded a first class degree in part 1B of the Medical Tripos this summer. Only recently the College had elected him to a Foundation Scholarship and had given him the prestigious Russell Vick Prize for Medicine.

They had climbed together in the Pyrenees, they had crossed Spitzbergen together and had been in Arctic Norway together. Three weeks ago they set off together for Mont Blanc, that evil mountain. They died together in a sudden and ferocious storm.

This awful news led me, therefore, to re-write this week's column but there are parts of the original which are still appropriate for what I also wrote earlier concerned the other side of belonging to a village community: the sharing not only of neighbourly triumphs but also of neighbourly tragedies. The Perretts have been but shortly in our midst but already the sense of shock at the death of their brilliant, adventurous young son spreads among us. Just as we greeted the news of James's many scholastic achievements so now we mourn with his family in their grief. It is a good thing to be a villager at a time of great trial and I pray that the Perretts will lean on us and gain strength from our togetherness.

I do not suggest that a village is the sole repository of feeling, that it monopolises the supply of shared sorrow. It is just that in small, slow places like ours we tend to involve ourselves in the minor misfortunes and passing griefs of others and are therefore somehow more prepared for the longer, lasting ones.

There will, of course, be many who will talk of the foolhardiness of young men and the dreadful waste. But what is youth without adventure? Where is fulfilment without achievement? The spirit stirs and rises up with risk. How many of us, crabbed with age, do not yearn for missed adventure, the prerogative of brave youth?

Birds, Bees and Cats

THE G-G-G-G-OWK

It was the call of a stuttering cuckoo which first gave me cause to reflect upon the utter joy of tranquility, a state of grace permitted to few of us in this noisy noisome world. Well, I like to think the bird was stuttering; if not it was either a case of hiccups or the demon drink. Anyway, herself and I were walking alone through our favourite bluebell wood just over the border in Suffolk some days ago when we first heard it. There was total peace in the huge wood, carpeted in trunk-to-trunk blue with infrequent smudges of white produced by the fragile and deliciously-named Field Mouse-ear (okay - Cerastium arvense, if you insist). Here was tranquility of a high order with only the snap of a dry branch under our feet and occasional rasping croaks from cock pheasants. But no man-made sound. No overhead drone of flying machine, no chuntering tractor, no cars, no trannies. But then our friendly gowk entered upon the sylvan scene with its "c-c-c-coo-coo". As we walked further into the fragrant wood the cuckoo followed us, its call remaining strong and clear as though it were tree-hopping to keep that odd-looking pair of humans in view. Vainly we searched the trees for a glimpse of him but as we left our vale of tranquility we laughed at his strange call which will doubtless haunt us down the dimming corridors of our memories.

IN MAJESTY'S PRESENCE

As a countryman I have long harboured a faint scorn for ornithology, regarding it as little more than the esoteric pursuit of the underprivileged townie, but all has changed with the unheralded arrival in our community of a magnificent and kingly visitor, for, on its migratory path from northern crags to sunny Africa, an osprey had been sampling the piscatorial sweet-meats of Swaffham Lode and sundry deep and delicious pike-filled pits.

Now the chance of spotting an osprey in the Fen is as likely as meeting a poor farmer and when news of his presence reached me I hurried off in that piece of tin which a salesman laughingly assured me was a motor car and proceeded, for reasons best known to the insurance company, to cause so much damage to the machine that the cheerful mechanics of Manchett's garage have been kept in busy employ ever since.

Thus, on my first hunt for the yellow-eyed fishing eagle my attention was somewhat distracted but determined not to let a few hundred quids' worth of damage deter me I continued my forays on foot. Fellow peasants in the village, luckier than me, have seen him in the very act of taking fish and they have watched him perched with pike-heavy beak for all the world like a proud desert monarch taking lunch. I have seen him in flight, once when I nearly mistook him for Jack heron as he floated with wings like cricket bats, his white tummy bright against a dark circle of trees and again, this time utterly unforgettable, in the heart of the silent fen with a crimson, sinking sun behind him. There, in that sublime quiet, just the two of us, and I felt again that inexplicable tingle which comes from being in the presence of majesty.

TEMPLE HAUNTERS

Never really felt sorry for a cuckoo before. Not until this morning, that is, this grey, dismal, doleful 13th day of May.

For I am newly returned from my pre-breakfast saunter down Fen Lane and though I went out accoutred as though for midwinter wild-fowling, all sweaters and waterproofs, yet still I managed to return bedraggled with damp and cold.

Which is why I sit worried about that poor old cuckoo. There he squats in the dripping woods over by Swaffham Prior Park, at the end of his vast migratory flight, and his two-note song comes stuttering over the swamped fields and I swear I have never head a more mournful, mopish, dejected bird.

Who can blame him? After crossing continents in his desperate urge to reach the jollities of a gentle, temperate English spring, he finds himself friz up to his nether parts and no chance at all of finding his favourtie nosh - a nice hairy caterpillar.

And down at Cow Bridge the martlets are back, skimming the water in their endless, effortless flight. Even they are flying with an unaccustomed degree of melancholy for they hate the cold. It bamboozles them and they, too, deserve better weather than this after their inward flight from distant and sunny climes.

I hope I do not hear you question the use of the word martlet!

For, as you must know, it is the heraldic term for the swift and those of you who have a martlet incorporated in your coat of arms will readily confirm that its presence there denotes that the original wearer of the distinction in your family served as a crusader pilgrim. (And those of you who don't have a coat of arms should nip out and get one sharpish).

The scholars among you will be aware of the name for this usually gayest of birds - their squeaks of delight when they hurtle up and down the village street are those of children newly released from the confinement of the classroom - and will immediately quote Banquo in Macbeth: "This guest of summer, the temple-haunting martlet."

SORRY, SORRY

A couple of yards from our back door where the asparagus bed begins, a pretty blue-grey cat languishes loudly. Whence it cometh we know not. In fact, we wot nothing of it at all except that very shortly it is likely to be in need of help from a feline psychiatrist because the poor fool has fallen for our own cat, Sebastian Herbert.

The strange new moggy spends hours in our garden waiting for that huge, useless lump of ours to make its appearance whereupon they sit eyeing each other happily, the newcomer purring with all the ardour of a love-lorn loon, obviously besotted. Nothing ever happens nor is it likely to. This strange courtship has never been shorn of innocence. They are as Adam and Eve before the fall, lovers bound by platonic bonds. And yet the lovely stranger has about her an aura of longing, a slight twinkle of lurking lust. And this is what worries me for I do believe we may have unwittingly led her towards presumptions which can never be fulfilled. You see, when we named our cat Sebastian Herbert it was before we had, er, checked up fully and it turned out that Sebastian H is in fact a she. And, following a visit to the vet, not much of a she either. Great expectations are about to be dashed.

SWANS BY THE HERD

Slid across the fens to the frozen wastes of Welney on Sunday afternoon with herself to have a gander at the birds there. Found the denizens of that distant empire all a-skating and a-sliding about and generally having a rare old time. We told ourselves how daft we were not to have taken our own skates with us and swore to return shortly to join in the fun which we so shall do.

Lovely, lovely scene. The sun, colour of a fresh egg yolk, takes a seeming eternity to drop off the edge of the ice sheet; the moon, palely loitering, comes up over our left shoulders; fenfolk of all ages and sizes are skimming over the shimmering ice, lissom and elegant as the finest corps de ballet. And glory heaped upon glory, overhead come herd after herd of Swans, rejoicing loudly at the prospect of tea laid out for them just behind us at the Wildfowl Trust headquarters. There is a mixed melody of four pieces of music - the beating of hundreds of wings, the red indian yelps of the Hooper swans, the scrunch of scores of skates and the crinkle-crankle of cracking ice.

We went off to see the birds eating. Then it was home. Crumpets toasted on the open fire. Plenty of butter. Honey from our own bees. Can't see why you live in the country, some twerp once said to me. It's so boring.

Mind you, whilst there is a grandeur in watching and listening to the vast choir of birds at Welney, I find just as much pleasure in the company of the pair of swans which live on our Lode just beyond Cow Bridge here in the village. I have spent hours watching them with their cygnets and now the cob and pen have ceased their once-angry hissing in my presence and they accept me with a tolerant wariness. I have many a chat with 'em when out walking before breakfast and they're very good listeners although entirely lacking in a sense of humour.

Indeed swans tend to be of a mournful nature despite the superstition which has persisted for centuries that they sing before death. It's an unfounded belief though you could have fooled Plato, Chrysippus, Aristotle, Euripides, Philostratus, Cicero, Seneca and Martial all of whom promulgated the idea. (And, of course, Shakespeare as well. As in Othello Act V, Scene 2: "I will play the swan, and die in music").

But I like 'em for their connection with that splendid group of people, the members of the Vintners' Company. They are among those who are granted the privilege of keeping a "game" of swans, a privilege which is manifested by the grant of a mark cut in the beak of their swans on the Thames. Their mark is two nicks in the form of a V which is why many delicious hostelries are called "The Swan with Two Nicks". Next time I enter a pub of that name I will raise my glass to the memory of that magnificent fenland afternoon and to my two lovely friends who dwell in peace under the shadow of Cow Bridge.

BEHIND THE VEIL

When I tell you that I have finally taken the veil do not leap rashly to the conclusion that I have renounced fleshly pleasures or that I have turned turtle and entered a nunnery. The veil in question is the traditional one of the bee-keeper and I bought mine this week from that doyen of apiarists, Bill Mead of Fowlmere, who displays an incredible wealth of tact, patience and sheer good humour with such idiot beginners in the bee lark as myself. I came to bees rather like hay goes to the horse - I was pitchforked into it by the machinations of that mad electrical contractor from Haslingfield, Bruno Konsiewicz. I call him mad because his middle European origins make him unnecessarily generous, and first he gave me a empty hive which, painted white, looked pretty in the orchard and, minus bees, was causing no trouble to anyone.

Then, to my utter horror, Bruno, the scourge of the golf club card tables, arrived with a huge swarm which he proceeded to instal in my hive before vanishing and leaving me to it. Hence the veil and many of the other tools of the craft which I now find so fascinating and soon, I hope, we will have our own honey for the ravening hordes I call my family. I will bring you more news of my bees which even now, despite the cold, are working the flowers of my three big lime trees. At least I hope they are mine and not those from the hives of that rotter Phil Coxhead at the other end of the village. He's been hanging about my garden a bit recently pretending to give me friendly advice about my stock of bees. I suspect he's been sussing out my limes for his own nefarious reasons. Kindly point your bees in the other direction Coxhead.

GARROTTED, DEPENDING......

Beset, as we are, by mammoth worries about the economy and jobs, and where the next florin is coming from, perhaps you will allow me to add to your miseries by telling two little tales. The first concerns a one-legged budgerigar kept briefly by the bewhiskered giant of the Cherryhinton Constitutional Club, Douglas Gibson. Its home was a gilded Victorian cage and, because of its infirmity, it was obliged to grasp its perch firmly with its one claw and lean for support against the ribs of the cage as though permanently pickled. It appeared content with its lot although I felt that its trill was somewhat muted.

The second concerns a memory I have from my youth in the Derbyshire hills of a peppery landowner who guarded jealously his valley pheasants and his moorland grouse and who placed, at strategic points on his estate, the following warning: "Trespassers will be garrotted or raped depending". These unconnected but true stories have blighted my bedtimes and dawns. For I cannot rid myself of these unanswerable questions - how did the budgie scratch itself? Did it wait until prying human eyes were averted, roll over on its back and indulge in an orgy of feather-fettling with its one claw? And what on earth did the old sportsman mean by "depending". Depending on what? Sex, age, the season, day of the week? I shall never know because bird and squire are long dead. But they haunt my dreams even now.

MAN WITH A DARK SECRET

Many men of huge talent have a secret, dark side to their lives, and occasionally it is the sad but necessary duty of the vigilant journalist to bare the truth as a public warning.

So, today I name and expose Terence Alexander Hawthorne English, internationally-famed heart transplant surgeon, member of the Society of Thoracic and Cardiovascular Surgeons of Great Britain and Ireland, father of four - and wanton breeder of useless kittens. Lurking in the depths of his home in Adams Road, Cambridge, is a cat of such startling feline fecundity that it produces litter upon litter and this is the point at which Terence English becomes a public menace. For, big softy that he is, he cannot put down any of the constantly arriving threats to household peace and he is therefore obliged, often under the guise of friendship, to foist them upon an unsuspecting world.

I should know. My dozy number three daughter, Naomi, was daft enough to become friendly with an English daughter. Result: two of their dratted kittens in this house within a couple of years. The first happily, sorry, sadly, bowled over by a kindly neighbour's car, had been trained apparently in its earliest infancy to leap from behind upon those who sit at typewriters and telephones. Once, as I spoke on the phone to a high-ranking clergyman of this city of Cambridge noted for his narrowness of mind in matters of language, the beast pounced upon me and the shock was such that I was obliged involuntarily to utter a phrase I learned when I was of the rude soldiery and which brought the telephone conversation to a peremptory conclusion.

Hearing of that kitten's demise the English mob lobbed yet another new-born kit in the direction of naive Naomi. This one, named, would you believe, Sebastian Herbert, drapes itself along my shoulders as I type. I cannot see what it is up to but the children swear it preens itself by using my shiny pate as a mirror. It is filled with a purring malevolence and behind its appealing eyes lies a hidden savagery. But I have a surprise for Mr English. Our latest kitten is misnamed. He is a she. And two can play at the English game....

"AND IS THERE HONEY....?"

And so to honey. This week, from the white hive half-hidden in the depths of the orchard, I harvested the first few pounds of glistening, glorious nectar produced by our happy bees in the first year of their employment by us. I can think of few more exciting, satisfying, utterly pleasing moments than that of finding viscid honey. I carried the first of my treasure to the kitchen table where ravening kids fell upon it with quickly muffled glad cries. I have other ideas than merely eating it and a pound or two will go to the making of mead, a pleasure of which I have dreamed ever since I read Thomas Wildman's directions for the production of mead with boiling water and the addition of hops to reduce the sweetness. Wildman wrote about it in perhaps the most famous aparian book, his "A Treatise on the Management of Bees", a second edition of 1770 which I have. But a neighbour of ours inherited a superbly bound first edition recently and it is my evil plot to ply her with my mead so that in a moment of light-headedness she will satisfy the lust I have for that book by selling it to me. Wildman would have approved of that ploy, methinks.

OUCH!

Well, it was inevitable. Last week my bees gave me a proper going over. I don't know if it was the peculiar weather or if it was due to the fact that I had cleared away some nettles near them - oh, yes, they actually become angry when people use shears to cut grass around the hive - but some of them penetrated my veil and my trousers and gave me a good old stinging. Still, I don't hold it against them and I shall persist.

INEXPLICABLE

Full forty years and more I have been a lover of birds; in woods, on moorlands, in peaty bogs, on high crags and under wide fenland sunsets of startling beauty. I have watched them, listened to them and, yes, shot quite a few of them. I have loved them for their glad colours, their sometimes plaintive, often playful calls, their merry music, the sweeping symmetry of their flight. And, not least, for the sport they provided and for their succulence at table. But every year as we edge into the glorious game shooting season I try to examine the seeming contradiction of the being who is at once a bird lover and a shooting man, the apparent inconsistency of killing and conservancy walking hand in hand through the countryside. Yet this is how it is and always was and the hardest shots have the softest hearts. Keen grouse men will spend as much time eulogising over the sad and plangent "quee quee" cry of a moorland curlew wading in a heather-girt bog as they will over "two dead in front and one behind". Hardened partridge men will break off yarning about a curling covey of redlegs to muse over the delights of a chorus of linnets singing from low bushes edging an old wood; music, I would add, which would lift the spirits of a bankrupt with a hernia. There is a phantom weirdness about field sportsmen which is not to be explained. The call of the gun is inescapable and inexplicable to those who heed not the lure of the outdoors. Out there under a brittle autumn sun or in a searing January gale there comes upon us a deepness of feeling for the English countryside which can be painful to the heart. The clean kill which all true field sportsmen seek is but a small part of that huge drama of the shoot composed of quest, surprise, field-craft and doom.

It was my old man who introduced me to birds and shooting for as a Derbyshire bobby he would take me as a child on long, lonely beat patrols for company. He showed me whirring blue-green kingfishers flashing along valley trout streams hovering occasionally over the water, a blurr of gaudy wings; herons flopping their languid way over the Duke's river to the fright of his fish and the fury of his bailiffs. Three hundred feet above, on the bare moors, he pointed to skeletal trees packed with unmoving grouse. He, too, could not resist the call of the gun and even now I cannot think of the old-fashioned policeman's cape without seeing in memory's eye the shot gun which invariably protruded from the one my father wore.

"I KILLED...."

Who killed cock robin? Sebastian Herbert, our cat killed cock robin, that's who. At least there were no sparrows' arrows around so I apportion the blame in the direction of our feline huntress. And not only killing him but laid him out all neat and tidy on the top step at our back door which is where she likes to present her trophies for our pleasure. Now robins, when they're not looking at you from Christmas cards, can be vicious little creatures given to much ill-will towards any bird which seeks the slightest morsel within their clearly defined empires. But this old robin was a great pal to me while I was gardening and I chatted to him for many a minute. When I rested he would sit on my spade looking at me as though to urge me on to fresh endeavours. Alas, gay robin is seen no more but the cat wears a plump and satisfied smile.

A GILDED CAGE

With not a lot better to amuse myself during that drenching thunder storm on Sunday I watched a line of house-martins bathing happily in the downpour. As they sat on a telephone wire above the kitchen window they were so pleased with themselves that they sang that gentle, twittering song of theirs whilst fluffing out every feather to let the torrential rain in. As they sang our budgerigar also burst into excited trills in his cage. Were they speaking to each other? Was our bird telling them how well off he is, safe from predators, constantly fed and watered and protected from the savagery of the elements? Or was he bemoaning his comfortable captivity as he listened to their tales of soaring freedom high over the kingdoms of the earth? I shall never know. But I do know that I worry about the caging of birds and we will never have another.

THE LION'S CAGE

A somewhat pathetic blackbird has attached itself to us and spends much of its time hopping in a desultory fashion around the back door waiting for scraps from the poor man's table. I throw it the odd piece of damp bread but I do so reluctantly not because I am anti clapped-out blackbirds but because I know that the great huntress of the fens, our cat Sebastian Herbert, lurks in the background and sure as blackbirds trill of a morning she will pounce and have him. I feel that my kindness is of a macabre and traitorous kind, rather like a favourite uncle taking a nephew to the zoo knowing full well they have left the lions' cage open.

LOONY DUNNOCK

Some of you asked why I said last week that one of my ambitions for the second fifty years of my life was to find a cuckoo's egg in a dunnock's nest. Why so, you asked? Because, I reply, I never managed to find one in the first fifty years. But why particularly in a hedge sparrow's nest? Because of all the nests wherein the cuckoo lays its parasitic eggs the dunnock's is the only one in which it does not bother to go through the miraculous business of mimicking the colouring of the host's own eggs. Cuckoo eggs have been found in more than 100 nests of different song-birds and always the cuckoo lays an egg which is similar in colour to that of its host. Sometimes their efforts at camouflage are so superb that their eggs are virtually indistinguishable from those of the host mother. Not so, however, when they drop in on the gentle dunnock and the cuckoo egg is patently alien amongst the natural blue eggs around it. Is it, I wonder, that the dunnock is colour blind? Is it too timid to argue? Or is it just plain loony?

HEN HARRIER AND SHOCK! HORROR!

Contrary to the belief of the average townie, the fens are packed with drama as I will now prove with the following tale of savagery and heartbreak in which a hunting hen harrier inadvertently brings about the downfall of a sad young man.

Some of you may recall that I have spoken in the past of our local worker in wood, one Ranald Scott, an import from Scotland, whose chief claim to local fame is that for some years now he has kept the secret of where the very best fenland mushrooms may be found. We have tempted him with flagons, tried trickery, followed him at morn and in the gloaming but the phlegmatic Scot kept his peace and gloated with great glee as he handed the delicacies around to the fuming locals.

Now, however, we come to last Sunday, a day of pleasing weather with gentle skies and colour setting the trees ablaze. Enter upon the scene Mr Ron Greenhill of the village of Reach who is out in the fen with his binoculars, he being a naturalist of considerable discernment. His glasses pick up the rare sight of a female hen harrier quartering a field of sugar beet, her owl-like face hardened by the urge to kill whatever game she can find. Ron watches fascinated and his glasses traverse the fen - then hallelujah, the powerful lenses pick out a stooping, furtive figure wearing the distinctive green and woolly-bobbled hat which marks the man out as our Ranald.

Yes, he's picking mushrooms: fat ones, wide-brimmed ones, some with stalks like pick handles. This discovery is the fenland equivalent of the opening of Joanna Southcott's Box, the breakthrough into Tutankhamun's tomb, the finding of Treasure Island. When the news is revealed to poor Ranald his initial disbelief turns to horror and horror to heartbreak and that to shock and we are obliged to pour pints of Greene King's best into him (though, to be truthful, by the amount of the stuff he normally sticks down his throat in the Oak it could be surmised that he is in a permanent state of shock). Still there is one consolation for the lad. Ron Greenhill knows where the magic patch is. Ranald knows. I know. And we ain't telling nobody - especially you lot out there.

All of which is really just an introduction to this part of the week's essay on the remarkable return to the fens of the lovely - albeit vicious - hen harrier, a breeder on moor and tundra, which, for some unknown reason has in the past eight years begun to winter in increasing numbers in our eastern flatlands. Tim Bennett, the sage warden at Wicken Fen, tells me that in the winter of 1977-78 there was a remarkably large influx of them into East Anglia; happily more came the following year and now research has shown that there are a number of communal and constant roosting sites in our own region.

Apparently they are dropping in on us from Scandinavia and central Europe though quite why seems to be a bit of a puzzle to the bird watchers. Obviously they enjoy our wide open spaces and I begin to wonder if, out of our barren grain prairies, we might have constructed a newly-welcoming environment for this exciting creature?

Mark you, when I talk about increasing numbers I'm not suggesting they are fluttering about in flocks. They are still a splendidly rare sight though there are three of them in Wicken Fen at the moment, one or two more floating - literally - around various nearby fens and, if you are idle like me, you may well catch an easy glimpse of one or two roosting just off the Quy roundabout outside Cambridge alongside Teversham Fen.

This year they've dropped in on us about a month earlier than in recent years and they'll be off again come March or April. Hope you see one before then. And should you happen to be an over-zealous game-keeper please leave 'em alone. I reckon there's enough game out here in our rich fields to share a partridge or two with a few smashing tourists like the hen harrier.

ONCE BITTERN

In gleeful anticipation of the day when suttee is introduced to these parts I am building a pile of sandalwood in the orchard and an event which befell me on Sunday afternoon brought that woman mate of mine closer to the pyre. As we walked through the gentle wilderness of Wicken Fen in search of those bitterns I mentioned last week I decided to test the thickness of the ice on the lode in the hope of an evening's skating. "Hold my hand, my dear", I said, all peace-ful-like, "while I try the ice". As I placed the not inconsiderable weight of my left leg upon the glassy surface she turned to watch an incoming flight of mallard and her hand missed mine. I plunged into the water and my oaths shattered the frozen silence causing horrified birds to rise and flee. As I slopped my way back to the car in water-filled welly the peals of laughter from the troll amazed a group of curious bird-watchers and through her tears she gasped something about "once bittern, twice shy" but I maintained a dignified and furious silence all the way home.

They Ol' Boys

OL' JOE CHAPMAN

Should your perambulations take you into Stow-cum-Quy perchance you will espy a small, weather-wizened man with bright eyes and a face like a pile of wet gravel. Fear not, for 'tis but kindly Joe Chapman, gamekeeper retired, and one so knowledgeable in the arts of the training of gun-dogs that some suggest he invented them. I have long suspected him of being both deeply religious and a health fanatic, since he is constantly in the company of Abbotts, albeit of the Greene King bottled variety and, since, for his health's sake, he has been taking a stiff, daily dose of Bell's ever since a florid sporting earl assured him in the shooting field that the liquid was, in fact, a Scottish anti-flu vaccine.

Now Joe is known to frequent, among others, a hostelry which stands a few yards from his cottage, and therein he is wont to mix with other village undesirables who, instead of joining in the new national sport of riot and looting, seek to engage themselves in other, stranger villainies. Thus it came to pass the other day that Joe, finding he had over-estimated the strength of his thirst by mid-lunchtime, was obliged to sleep off the overquench.

The lads he left behind, mindful of that undeniable law of nature which states that if ten pints go down the throat some of it is bound to seek its way out again very shortly, gave Joe half an hour in his kip and then scratched his bedroom window with a flue brush. Awakened, the inevitable happened and Joe rushed for the relief of his outside lavatory. The lads sat back in the bushes as Joe, still somewhat bleary of thought and action, found the tiny building blocked entirely by the presence of one very large, black nanny-goat. He fled elsewhere with his pressing problem, to the loud hoots of his drinking pals. But he had the last laugh. For while 'tis easy enough to push a nanny-goat into a small space with an inward-opening door, 'taint so easy getting her out again. And while the lads sweated and strained trying to budge the old girl Joe had time to nip down the road to try just one more glass...

And Joe tells me there is a moral here. "Always remember", says he, "you can take a little piggy to market but don't ever take an old nanny to the loo".

OL' JIM BORLEY

So I'm sitting in the Oak relaxing with a pint after a hard day's thinking when in strolls trouble in the form of big Jim Borley. He tends to create domestic mayhem whenever he enters the hallowed interior of a public house because all intentions of going home for an early supper are abandoned as soon as he starts talking since the fact is that Jim Borley is one of those characters whose company is impossible to quit until the tears of laughter leave you so weak you are obliged to seek the sanctuary of home. He is now in his 84th year though when he burst into song the other night, a scotch and a glass of Abbot ale before him and a fat cigar in his hand, a stranger might have been forgiven for halving his age for the lungs which belted out "The Lincolnshire Poacher" are as powerful as the bellows he has worked with through his long life. Jim has been a blacksmith over at Teversham these past 69 years and although he has given up shoeing horses he still turns out a pretty piece of ironwork for his friends. He is the sort of bloke that town-bred writers tend to invent and there is about him something of a world we will never see again. He was born in a pub like his father before him and it seems that ale, work and singing have been the three major ingredients of his life. He reckons that as a young man in his smithy in Teversham he used to work up an almighty thirst because from his furnace he could see the landlord pulling pints in the pub across the road and since he always sang as he hammered away on his mighty anvil there were times when the pints fairly sizzled down his throat. He is famous for his renderings of Gilbert and Sullivan's more complicated pieces and he treated us to some of them in the Oak in between his many tales ... like how, in the 39 years he was a part-time parish constable he never made an arrest. "Always used to take 'em down to the Rose and Crown and settle the argument there", he gurgled.

"They never seemed to want to argue with me". Maybe one reason for the early acquiescence of local troublemakers was that Jim's favourite trick when real policemen visited his smithy was to sit them on his four hundredweight anvil and carry them across the road. And if you don't believe that call on him next time you are in Teversham, shake him by the hand and see if you can extricate yourself from his grip before he decides to let you go. Our Jim is built like a brick malt house and is still immensely fit despite having had six major operations, the first of which was for peritonitis and as Jim puts it: "At the time I was so full of Guinness and bitter that I came round while the surgeons were still sawing away". Alas, the days are gone when Jim helped out local vets by sitting on the head of a ton and a half stallion calming it with a bag of chloroform while they operated at the other end and maybe he won't be throwing that old anvil around any more. But Jim, 69 years a chorister, is still singing and drinking and smoking and working and when I finally left the Oak the laughter he was creating followed me down the dark and stormy street.

OL' SNOWY CHALMERS

Hacked over to Newmarket to renew my acquaintanceship with the racing game after an enforced absence due mainly to the persistent interference in my financial affairs by a humourless Collector of Taxes and to a bank manager who has a weird notion that his customers should be required to pay something into their accounts now and again.

Ignoring their latest anguished demands I made a foray once more into that temple of optimism where the faithful punters watch their hopes fly around in ever decreasing circles until they finally disappear into the bookies' satchels and I can report that nothing has changed during my absence. The same efficient girls still dispense some of the most expensive drinks in England in the Members' bars, the bookmakers still bemoan their constant losses.

Nowhere can there be such dramatic personality changes as at the racecourse - I turned my glasses from watching one race to studying the faces of the punters and I picked out a familiar craggy Cambridge face which became so filled with evil greed as his horse moved through to take up the running that I realised for the first time exactly what Dorian Gray must have seen when he finally unveiled his own portrait. Yet I gladly shared his champagne after the race and found he had reverted to his usual charming and witty self. Strange what gambling does to a man.

But what pleased me most was to find waiting to greet me - and his many other sporting friends - that most remarkable of racing men, Cambridge's own David "Snowy" Chalmers. Snowy surveys the

Newmarket scene immutable as the Devil's Dyke, and with over 70 years experience he is now one of the world's greatest experts on two things: horseflesh and champagne. Indeed, he attacks a bottle of wine with the sort of ferocity normally reserved for a midnight mugger, particularly if it is the gift of a grateful friend. His admitted fondness for the fizz was once almost his final undoing as he delights in telling. Having overdone the guzzle once at York racecourse he fell from the top end of the stand and damaged himself so much he woke up in hospital. In the next bed lay a huge man, heavily bandaged. He regarded Snowy with unfeigned malignancy. Snowy enquired the reason for his unfortunate presence to which the large neighbour, through gritted teeth, muttered: "I was minding my own business, watching the race, when some idiot fell on me from the top of the stands. And when I get these bandages off......"

No coward, but a man of great commonsense, Snowy forthwith discharged himself from hospital and limped quietly back to Cambridge.

OL' GIBBIE

Heaven, it is said, awards the vengeance due and it certainly seemed like a gift from the gods when last week an opportunity arose which allowed me to exact a joyful revenge from a man who has outwitted me these past 25 years.

Douglas Gibson is his name, formerly of Royston and now of Fulbourn in this county. A large man is Master Gibson, in stature, appetites and thirsts and I have oft times rued the day we met.

For, you see, it's like this. Gibbie and I have roistered through the eastern counties together for a quarter of a century. He is a great countryman and his knowledge of his native Suffolk and of his adopted Cambridgeshire is immense.

He knows of a way of life now, alas, vanished from our villages but he also knows where the best hams are still prepared, where a discreet knock on the back door will open up a pub out of hours, where the plumpest hares are to be found, the heaviest pheasants, the frothiest beers. He can smell a rare piece of beef at a thousand yards and some sixth sense tells him when the oyster is at its juiciest.

He is the acknowledged master of the wassail, the carousal. He is a walking feast, a revelling Bacchus. And, to boot, a kind and gentle man.

But for 25 years he has been thieving from me. It gives him enormous and continuing pleasure to remove by subtle and cunning means any goodies which other kind-hearted souls have intended for my own delectation.

If Tubby Edwards leaves me a jar of his magnificent homemade curried pickle for collection in the Cherryhinton Constitutional Club and Gibbie gets there first - it disappears. When we shot together in Norfolk somehow my pheasants would always vanish from my car boot on the homeward journey. A half dozen duck eggs from Peter Clappison; they too would evaporate if Gibson was around.

Once I brought a splendid hand-raised pork pie back to Cambridge from Stamford. It never reached home and days later Gibbie told me it was the tastiest he had eaten for many a long day. When Gordon Laurie presented me with a lavish gift of a side of delicately pink salmon smoked by the Queen's smoker up in wildest Caledonia, Gibbie and some of his other mates choked with laughter as they scoffed it after nicking it from my car.

The examples could go on for ever.

But, ho ho, last week it was my turn. Kindly John Robinson from Babraham trotted into town bearing large quantities of that rarest and most delicious of country delicacies, the morel or spring mushroom.

To Master Gibson the morel is immensely superior to the finest truffle. He bleats with pleasure when he eats them. They are the pinnacle of his gastronomic year.

Yes, well. John Robinson handed the treasured morels to me so that I might pass them on to my old mate Gibbie later that day. It now gives me pleasure on a massive scale to admit that I stole those morels. I pinched 'em with malice aforethought, brazenly and happily. I took 'em home and I chortled with 25 years of bottled up glee as I cooked 'em in butter and lemon juice. I ate 'em three breakfasts running. The missus and I noshed 'em at dinner.

Master Gibson, they were superb and I reckon we are almost quits.

OL' MAURICE WRIGHT

Meandering down the fen I bumped into the old boy Maurice Wright, whose sense of logic is as immaculate as his garden. Talk turned to partridges, which are pairing off nicely, and he told me how greedy they were once his greens started showing. I sympathised, knowing how much effort goes into his neat plot, but he spurned my sympathy, saying he welcomed their occasional appearance and, with a sly smile, he uttered a devastating truism: "Always remember, bor, there's more gravy in a partridge than there is in a 'tater". Irrefutable!

OL' JONAH

Never been so pleased to buy anyone a whisky as I was for a retired poacher of great renown who called in at the local on Sunday night. Old Jonah Osborne was the man, at 84 his poaching days behind him and a little wobbly on the legs (which on reflection was probably due to the generosity of others before me). Jonah was born into poverty and a family of ten in a cottage, which still stands, in Quarry Lane, Swaffham Bulbeck, left school at ten and, until he took the King's Shilling and went for a soldier, was to cause many sleepless nights for gamekeepers on the big estates around his home.

Jonah lives foreign now, over at Glemsford in Suffolk, but kind friends brought him back to his former village and the pub where he took his pints over 60 years ago. He chortled and drank his way through his long-ago memories of how he played fox to the keepers' hounds. He had taken birds from Squire Allix at Swaffham Prior, from Mr Hick's estate at The Temple in Great Wilbraham and, later, from Lord Fairhaven at Anglesey Abbey. And he had been caught at the caper, he said, far too many times he had been caught. "Always ended up in the old court house at Bottisham charged with the same thing. They got fed up with me down there. Even had a cousin from Stow-cum-quy on the bench there once and he fined me £17. That didn't half sting, that did".

His tales were told as of a countryman remembering times we shall never see again. He was not boasting of theft; his poaching, unlike that of the criminal, motorised poacher of today, who steals for financial gain, was more of a nocturnal game, a bent country craft. It was one for the pot, not ten brace for the wallet. Well, perhaps just the occasional little profit, like the time before the Great War when he helped the village baker.

"He was a bit tight with his cash was the old boy and he asked me once if I would get him an old hare for his supper. I took one down to this very pub where he was sitting a-drinking and said he could have it for a florin. No, said he, it was wet and scruffy and looked like it had been lying out in the field. So I takes the old hare home, dries him in front of the fire, brushes his old coat nice and tidy-like. Then I takes him to the Oak next night and tells the baker I have a fresh-killed one and bigger than the other which he can have for half a crown. He pays up promptly and buys me a drink so I diddled him out of a tanner. I always laugh when I think on it."

I gave him glad tidings. They had closed down the old court house at Bottisham, I said. His fading eyes lit brightly at the news and, briefly, there was a glint of foxy ambition about him as of yore. "Danged good thing too", he beamed as he said his farewells.

OL' BEAN MAN

And talking of broad beans I bumped into an old mate in the Wheatsheaf in Stow-cum-Quy recently and he told me a little tale which I pass on with pleasure. Seems he knew an ancient old boy over at Great Wilbraham who grew broad beans of such immense size and such palatable flavour that they were the envy of the parish, nay of several parishes around. The old man, in the way of wily gardeners, would not reveal the name of his beans, nor would he part with any seed. They were his one great achievement in life and hard luck to everybody else. The old boy inevitably reached his time in life and knowing the end was near my friend visited him and finally asked him to reveal the truth about the famous broad beans. The old gardener asked: "Can you keep a secret?" "Yes, yes, of course I can", said my friend. "Well", croaked the old 'un. "So can I".

OL' JOE'S FAREWELL

For no apparent reason the great Cedar of Lebanon which graced the elegant frontage of Quy Hall these past 140 years suddenly keeled over and died last Friday morning. At roughly the same time as the huge tree fell so, at the other end of the gracious Park, little Joe Chapman failed for once to rise from his bed and he too passed on.

Old Joe wasn't quite as ancient as the Cedar though upon occasions his craggy visage suggested to onlookers that perhaps, after all, he might have shared a similar birthdate with the splendid tree, particularly after one of his better nights in the Wheatsheaf or the White Swan of his beloved birthplace of Stow-cum-Quy.

It would be fanciful to debate whether the tree died from sympathy at Old Joe's death or t'other way round though I like to think that the tree was making a final sad sacrifice for undoubtedly they were long-standing mates. Fact is, Old Joe must have known just about every tree on the Quy Hall estate for as the former gamekeeper for the Francis family he watched generations of saplings climbing into maturity as he taught generations of Francis children to shoot and to learn the quiet secrets of their woodlands and hedgerows.

Old Joe was nothing much to look at being only slightly larger than a reasonably-fed garden gnome yet he was one of those small and seemingly unremarkable blokes who could without bombast or intrusion become the immediate centre of conversation wherever sporting folk foregathered.

Old Joe stuck to the village of his birth and keepered the estate until there came a misunderstanding with old Colonel Francis which led to a temporary parting of the ways but such is life in these places that Old Joe stayed on in his tiny cottage at the end of the Avenue leading to the Hall and retained the family's friendship and not all the black horses of hell could keep him from his former wanderings over the broad acres. Indeed, it would be unwise and untruthful to suggest that Old Joe was without sin in his profession and when I meet up with him in due course he will not chide me, I hope, for suggesting that occasionally a Francis pheasant or partridge might just have found its way into Old Joe's personal pot.

To talk to Old Joe was to live in another world at another time for he knew well the old and unrepeatable days of game shooting before the last war and his tales were both a delight and a revelation. He loaded for shots like the Queen's late father, for Lord Mountbatten, for the sporting Maharajahs. He could not, however, stand rotten shots. To one such over at Great Wilbraham who constantly pricked his pheasants and who repeated: "Watch that one Chapman. It's sure to come down", Old Joe finally said: "The only time they'll come down is when they're hungry."

The ease and facility with which he was able to train the most recalcitrant of gundogs was only slightly less miraculous than the manner in which he was able to convert the contents of a bottle of malt whisky into an arid void and many is the time I have seen a strange, inner light shining forth from his twinkling eyes after a day's shooting followed by the taking of a dose of his favourite syrup.

I see him now, game bag over his shoulder, dog at his heel, marching off to the fields with maybe a stop at the pub on the way. They bury Old Joe in the churchyard of his native village on Friday, the day I had chosen to visit this year's Game Fair at Broadlands. I cannot now go to Hampshire for I intend to say "Cheers" to the loveable rascal, to Old Joe the one-off job, the ulimate village character.

Just wish they'd had time to line his coffin with cedar wood.

OL' "FERRET"

I've had many a pint in many a pub with a fiendish friend whose pleasure it was - and, mayhap, still is - to shock and startle other customers with his habit of stuffing ferrets down his trousers and up his shirt. From Norfolk to his home village of Shelford I have laughed at the looks of sheer astonishment on the faces of the unwary as his fearsome pets appeared from the most peculiar parts of his attire and it is with some sadness that I realise how long it is since I shared a merry moment or two with him in coney-filled hedgerow or chatter-stuffed bar. He is known to the civilised workd as Dennis Howard but to the rapscallions of the sporting domain he is called simply and obviously "Ferret", a title which clings to him as tenaciously as would his half-tamed polecats hang on to a strange finger poked in their direction. He springs to mind because the ancient sport at which he has so long excelled is once again reviving after years of neglect in country patches. Ferreting is returning to popularity for two very good reasons: there are increasing numbers of brer rabbit for in many areas the animal has successfully fought off the ravages of myxemetosis and is becoming once more a pretty but undeniably scavenging member of the countryside population. And discerning housewives are remembering or learning about the culinary delights of this succulent little beastie. (And if you think only in terms of rabbit pie, think again. Mrs Beeton has more than 30 recipes for rabbit dishes.) So the ferrets are out and about again and the lads who take themselves off for a day's rabbiting in the manner of their forefathers can only be applauded for they are rewarding themselves with free sport, they are ridding the farmer of his unwelcome guests, providing splendid and healthy fare for many a table and, with rabbits fetching around a quid each from grateful butchers, providing themselves with enough beer money to nip off to their local where, with a little bit of luck, they might bump into a real character who could tell 'em a thing or two. Like my old mate "Ferret".

OL' ALVAH

Scuttle the portholes, let steeple bells ring, fling caviar to the cat and open the last of the champers - I've finally done it. And not once but thrice. Yup, in front of witnesses I won three out of three games of cribbage against the king, nay, the emperor of the crib board, old Alvah Badcock of Reach. It is he, some of you may recall, who for years has been cycling down to the Oak from his fenland home in the certain knowledge that he will extract a fistful of florins from me in the course of a game or several. I cannot recall ever beating him despite recourse to fervent prayer, the application of strong liquor and even an accidental (ho ho) overpegging to my own advantage. But t'other day in full view of his life-long chum Percy Blinco I devoured him, humbled him and brought the edifice of his reputation crashing down around his glass of shandy with my three victories. As folk in these parts will tell such a feat is the equivalent of climbing the north face of the Eiger with hands and feet bound or swimming the channel in a lead suit. Now I have been lifted up and shown all the kingdoms of the earth and it's no use my old mate Alvah hanging around the Oak hoping for revenge 'cause I've retired from the game while I'm at the top and not playing any more, so there!

OL' JOHN MEDLICOTT

As I write the ship of state is tilting slightly as the national water strike weighs anchor and it behoves all civic minded citizens to take their whisky straight until the crisis is resolved. The nation faces hardships but in my view any problems which arise in the fens can be blamed not upon the water workers but upon Cornelius Vermuyden and his gang of Dutch drainers who came over here and turned our boggy fens into rich farmland in the 17th century. If they had but left well alone we could all be living on stilts surrounded by the best shooting and fishing in Europe and up to our armpits in water so that we could thumb our noses at the massed ranks of stikers who now infest the Anglian Water Authority. Not that the strike worries me terribly for I have the same view of water as Chesterton who told us that Noah often said to his wife when he sat down to dine "I don't care where the water goes if it doesn't go into the wine". So turn off the taps, dig out a few bottles of the elderberry or the parsnip and lock yourselves in till it's all over.

Kipling too had something to say about water as you will recall. Although he was talking about slaughter he declared "you will do your work on water and you'll lick the bloomin' boots of 'im that's got it." Well, we're a bit short on Gunga Dins around these parts but talking of strikes and boot-licking brings me immediately to John Medlicott of Burwell who, in his poultry rearing days, was more likely to have bitten a trade unionist's leg off than to have licked his footwear. John and his wife died within a day of each other and were buried together last week. Although we were deeply saddened by their passing many of us remember him and his astonishing actions of some years ago with grim amusement bordering on admiring pride. For it was John Medlicott who earned himself immortal local fame when he took on the whole might of the Electrical Trades Union. As a struggling poultry man he had just fought off the rampages of fowl pest only to find that the electricians were calling a series of stikes which meant that his electrically heated chicken sheds were constantly at risk. Now John was a fenman bold and blunt and having spent four of the war years as a disgruntled guest of Emperor Hirohito and his merry mob he was in no mood to have his peacetime livelihood dashed by the activities of his strking countrymen. Indeed, he felt he had a right and duty to deliver an opinion or two about those who were ruining him, albeit inadvertently. He proceeded to express himself in spectacular fashion. Knowing that some electricians had parked their cars over by the Burwell power station he loaded his spraying machine with liquid chicken manure, hitched it to his tractor and without more ado sprayed the offensive mixture over the cars heedless of whether their windows were open or not. News of his precipitate action spread to the metropolis and John agreed to participate in a David Frost TV debate on the subject. But when he duly came face to fizzog with senior members of the ETU it was more than John could stand and in a twink he had his old coat off and was all for giving those Londoners a good duffing over. He was restrained, alas, and then there was talk of the cockney electricians moving into the fens to sort John out. The police put an end to that nonsense although I suspect that with the joyful aid of one or two of his mates from Reach and around it might have been the best punch-up since they built the Devil's Dyke. Now, I have nothing at all against either electricians or water workers and of course we must all fight our battles within the confines of the law. But the thought of one man standing alone against the big battalions fills me with delight in this dreary boot-licking world and for the memory of your glorious stand John Medlicott I raises my glass to you and long may your type flourish out here in the dry fens where no water is.

OL' DICK CAMPS

So it rained stair rods on St Swithin's Day last week and that wiped the grins off a few farmers' faces. Still it allowed Dick Camps to slide away from his soaked fields for an hour in order to drop a pint in the Three Tuns at Abington where by chance I had called to rest my weary self on the arduous journey from Linton to Cambridge. We fell to talking about harvests past and Dick, whose cap has been worn at a rakish milking position for twenty years to my knowledge, told me of a neighbouring farmer on the Gogs who attended harvest festival with a somewhat troubled mind. At the end of the lustily sung line "All is safely gathered in" the congregation was startled by a strange and resonant grunt from the rear of the church. At the service's end the vicar inquired diligently of the neighbour as to the reason for the odd noise. The farmer replied that he wanted to be quite certain that anyone up there who might have been listening should be in no doubt about his own personal position and after 'safely gathered in' he had added for good measure: "Bar the beans".

OL' HARRY REEVES

Met one of the great fishmongers at the weekend. Bumped into Harry Reeves whose fish and chip shop at Burwell was a glutton's delight and whose fresh wet fish turned every day into a Friday. Long retired, he's lost none of his sparkle. I asked him how old he was now and he told me solemnly: "About 77, boy. Would have been 78 but I got laid up with the measles for a time".

OL' HAROLD SENNITT

Occasionally there is a forceful rap on my back door and there on the doorstep is my favourite fenman, a wicked smile on his craggy face and, inevitably, a bag of goodies - plump onions, sweet carrots or giant potatoes - in his powerful grip. He slides out of his wellies and while he waits for his cuppa he natters on something wonderful. This week he arrived bearing six sacks of dried peat ready for the fire for Harold Sennitt is the last of the fenland peat diggers, as nifty a wielder of the spade and beckett as you are ever likely to see. (Indeed, the only user of the latter tool you will see around here). He is a man of the lonely places and I first met him years ago skating out on the frozen washes near Upware, where, on his long fen skates, this pear-shaped little man dazzled us with the delicacy of his flowing movements. He's a handy man with a gun and the locals tell the tale of the day a syndicate of Cambridge doctors were out shooting near Harold's patch of land over by Reach Lode. After walking for miles and bagging little the frustrated doctors found Harold standing on his own piece of black fen soil festooned with pheasants and partridges which he had shot as they flew on ahead of the townies. With his ebony eyes atwinkle he asked in his innocent drawl if anyone could let him have a few cartridges as he seemed to have fired all his! I doubt if there is anything Harold doesn't know about fur and feather and there is danged little he doesn't ken about the old ways of life in the fen. Although he won't admit it he is getting on a bit now and because he has not been feeling a thousand per cent his doctor has told him to take life easier but that's like telling the Cam to flow backwards and that is why he was out lugging peat around the other day. He is putting on a special show come June for about 80 lucky kids from schools at Fen Drayton, Papworth and Elsworth who will watch him digging peat near the banks of Wicken Lode. I hope they pay attention for the memory will live with them until they can tell their grandchildren of the old man of the fens. By then Harold will have long ago cut his last, damp brick and I will have had my last comfy doze in front of a gentle peat fire.

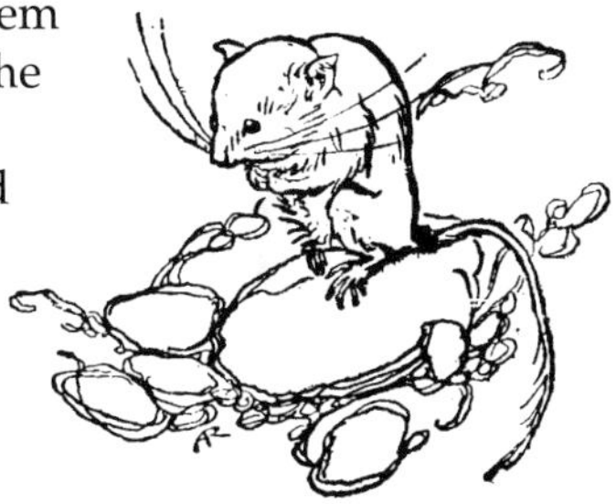

Sam, the World's Worst Gundog

SPORT, FOOD AND WOMEN

After being with me for eleven years my old dog Sam, the Worst Gundog in Europe, has developed a limp. It's designed, of course, to produce an unwarranted display of sympathy on my part so that I should finally show some form of friendship. But I've rumbled him and I know he's faking because whenever he sees a village moggy, a hare or a rat or whenever there is a chance of a spare meal or catching up with a lady hound he puts on a sprint which would win him the Greyhound Derby. Sport, food and women, that's all the damn dog thinks about. Can't imagine where he gets his ideas.

THE ARISTO

I admit to being slow on the uptake and it seems that it has taken me 12 years to understand why that crazy canine friend of mine, dopy Sam, the World's Worst Gundog, is so independent of mind when I suggest to him a certain course of action. It's something to do with his aristocratic breeding. For example, if I shout "heel", he swings his old head round and fixes me with a quizzical stare before ignoring me and continuing on his pre-determined course. I've always thought it was pure disobedience but the truth flashed in on me t'other day when he again shamed me in front of some people who have real dogs. It's quite simple and not really his fault. I now understand that when I call "heel" he obviously takes it more as an accusation than a command and being a Labrador of high birth he chooses to be disdainful of the coarsely-shouted insult.

NOT WORTH SEVEN AND A TANNER

There's talk this week of abolishing the present dog licence and replacing it with a ten quid job and when I mentioned this casually to my dog Sam, the World's Worst Gundog he curled his lip and assumed a very hang-dog expression if he will forgive me for using such a term. He is well aware, you see, that he is not worth even the current seven and a tanner licence for in the thirteen years he has haunted the lives of the family Jeacock he has brought nothing upon us other than shame, embarrassment and ignominy. He is haughty and aristocratic for his sires roamed the Sandringham estate and his brethren are there to this day. Indeed the full title which he carries upon his impeccable pedigree is "High Shot of Bulbeck", a monicker which, though suitably pompous for him, is somewhat difficult to bellow in a crowded street. The kids re-christened him Sambo but what with the race relations act and all that there were further public complications so he became plain Sam and upon reflection I wonder if that rather common name upset the youthful canine grandee and was the cause of his lifelong waywardness. For Sam has become a legend in his own time and on shoots in five counties he has left behind him a string of infuriated gamekeepers and scores of tittering shooting men delighted at his master's discomfort. I persisted with him over the years because as a retriever of game he is magnificent and his nose would have made him a champion. Alas and alack his sense of smell is the only sense he ever developed and both commonsense and obedience are unknown factors in his life. Despite a rigorous training he grew into a hound of strong-willed self-determination and though I have tried everything from words of stern command to whimpering entreaties he goes his own way oblivious of expected decencies. He is very much a village joke; or rather he has made me a laughing stock and small boys guffaw as he ignores my pleas to come to heel. Mind you, he isn't daft and he is fully aware of that power to which Kipling referred when he wrote: "Brothers and Sisters, I bid you beware of giving your heart to a dog to tear" and he plays upon our heartstrings with all the subtlety of a Menuhin. But now, at last, I believe I have him. I merely need to wave a tenner at him and he becomes compliant and fawning, desperately anxious to justify any increase in the cost of his licence.

OL' GREYBEARD`

Were there ever two such perfect days as last Saturday and Sunday? Overnight frosts left sparkling skies throughout the day and I wished I could have bottled the air, it was so fresh and invigorating. As I limped off down the fen road with ancient Sam, the World's Worst Gundog, we nattered about it being the finest season of the year. Though when I became poetic about mists and fruitfulness the old fool ignored me but his grizzled grey muzzle showed a snicker of approval when I told him that, in honesty, what I really love about autumn is that I don't need to mow those damned lawns again for a long, long time.

MASTER?

I'm ambling down a wide drove with decrepit Sam, Fenland's Worst Gundog, when from the edge of a field of barley flops an apparently distressed partridge, not red-legged but of the English variety. She lands twenty yards ahead of us uttering a high-pitched "keev-it", one wing flapping brokenly. She is performing that ageless and incredibly brave decoying action of deliberately attracting our attention to draw us away from the nest she has just left. Of course she is perfectly fit and when she considers her nest to be safe from man and dog she hurtles away in a blurring whirr followed by a long, low glide. Sam is utterly unimpressed and turns to me with a look written over his grey-muzzled face which says quite clearly: "We've seen it all before" and we stroll on, master and friend, though which of us is which I'm blessed if I can soundly declare.

GREAT-UNCLE CLARENCE

My old dog Sam, the Worst Gundog in England, is nearing the end of his days and recently he has been so hang-dog and miserable I thought I would have to face the unthinkable. Then, two days ago, a young lady hound in the village found herself in an interesting condition and suddenly, from being utterly decrepit, the beast put a new spring into his step. Now, his nose shines, the great head is alert and he hurtles out of the door like a puppy. He reminds me perfectly of my late great-uncle Clarence who, deep into his eighties, threw away his crutches, took up his bed, so to speak, and married a lass forty years his junior. He died two months after the wedding but, like old Sam, he spent his last days with a smile on his face.

"BE NOT BEGUILED"

Went for a walk in a half gale with daft Sam, the World's Worst Gundog. Actually, it was more of a sluggish saunter because nothing will make the old fool quicken his pace unless it be bitch or bunny. Yet he makes the perfect walking companion for long ago he mastered the art of conversation which is, of course, to keep quiet while the other bloke blathers on. He understands my every word though now, as over the 13 years of his life, he tends to ignore my more important passages, particularly my stiff and stern words of command. We shuffled along on that day last week when we were bathed in a strong but soft west wind. The poet claims that the west wind's a warm wind full of birds' cries but there were no birds' cries in our gale as it wrapped us round in hypocritical winter warmth. Just the sound of creaking joints on elderly trees, a whistling in the wires and a constant, ululating moan as of a choir of owls. As we strolled on in perfect harmony I addressed the canine loon in this wise: "Sam", quoth I, "be not beguiled by this gentle gale for I have lived more winters than you have enjoyed wholesome dinners and in callow youth-hood I learned that the weather has the fickle wiles of a beautiful woman. Its warm caresses will weaken your resolve and without cunning caution you will be unprepared for the chill change which is certain to follow; and I detect an inconsistency in the air, my old friend, so prepare yourself for before Yuletide ends there will come a great wind out of the east, a veritable Genghis Khan of a blast, all cruel and vengeful. It will bear upon its vicious breath a freezing snarl which will curl the grey hairs of your aged muzzle and rattle your stiffening joints. So enjoy the balmy day, my lad, for 'twill soon be ended". He pretended not to be listening but I know he heard my message for he thereupon turned his weary tail and led me back to our fireside before the change came about.

SILLY OLD FOOL

Had to collect some pills for old Sam from that excellent vet over at Soham who must be a reader of this column for he marked the packet with the inscription: "For Sam, the World's Worst Gundog". The silly old fool, the dog not the vet, seemed to appreciate the joke for he's halfway to getting better already.

POOR OL' BOY

Last week son Simon and I were getting ourselves geared up for a stroll down the fen with the guns when Sam, the Worst Gundog in the Common Market, began to tremble and whine. He is too decrepit to face the rigours of a day's shooting and 'twould be cruelty to inflict such exercise upon his aged and aching limbs. Yet to deny him the pleasure of joining us as of yore was in itself a form of cruelty and his anxiety to be off was pitiful to behold. The sight of the guns drove him to a frenzy of begging and as we strode off in the rain his whimpers followed us and we were deeply sorrowful for the old lad.

FEAST OF MEMORIES

My old dog Sam may be the Worst Gundog in the World but he carries his sporting shame with an air of aristocratic disdain, a canine hauteur which suggests that though he may have let the side down he is nevertheless immensely well-bred, a swank, a swell. So I watched him with interest as he lay at his ease on the lawn, a light breeze playing around his head. He lifted his greying muzzle to catch the eddying scents of lady dogs in the village. There was a suggestion of a snicker about his mouth as he caught the lovely smells of his youth and for all the world he looked exactly like an aged roue sitting by the open window of his London club watching the gels stroll by and feasting upon vaguely stirring memories.

ALAS! POOR VINTNER

So, to a cautionary warning that the pursuit of selfish pleasure can be disastrous. I relate the tale without relish and with considerable rancour. With my family happily snow-bound in Yorkshire at the weekend I plan a simple undisturbed evening before the fire in my study. My last bottle of Chateau Leoville-Las-Cases 1969 - "a fair but uneven year", say the experts, but to me "superb" since I have no more - sits haughtily in its decanter on the low table at my elbow, a plate of the first asparagus from the garden accompanied by a smudge of slightly garlicky mayonnaise on a plate on my lap, apple and cherry logs a-splutter in the grate and Sir Pelham Warner's history of Lord's within reach to be re-read.

Suffused with pleasurable anticipation I stroke the greying muzzle of old Sam (The Worst Gundog In England) who, astonished at such unaccustomed kindness, stretches creakily to his feet and with a delighted swish of the tail, knocks the decanter over, converting the vintner's noblest product into a mere carpet stain. I stride through the storm to the pub and order a pint of bitter. With vinegar crisps.

FAREWELL, OLD SAM

Our dog Sam, the World's Worst Gundog, is no more. His strange and splendid life came to an end early on Sunday morning before the village was astir and now he lies under a gnarled apple tree in the orchard where he idled away so many of his sunny days. He is surrounded by the pristine beds of snowdrops and golden aconites of this fresh spring and is content.

Our dog Sam was a black labrador of nearly 14 years but that bare statement is as frugal as describing a glorious oak as a piece of timber. No, he was much, much more than just another black labrador.

Our dog Sam really was the most awful gundog ever to roam these broad Eastern acres of ours yet he had a mysterious ability to invest his waywardness and crass public behaviour with such a sense of joyous enthusiasm that it was impossible not to join in the general laughter which seemed to follow him through the years of his indiscretions.

Our dog Sam floundered through mire and stream, panted through tangled undergrowth and slipped and scurried over heavy plough to retrieve game which fell to my gun over a decade.

But he was totally wilful, utterly uncontrollable and, eventually, I was obliged to shoot with him alone since to offer him a day's sport on an organised shoot was to court obloquy and ridicule.

He could - and would - empty a well-stocked pheasant covert with a crashing, barking dash through the brambles and sometimes I harboured suspicions that perhaps he was on the side of the quarry.

Thus our dog Sam became my sole companion in lonely places when we went after duck and pigeon, pheasant and partridge, hare and rabbit and under lowering winter skies I was able to laugh openly at his bungling but ambitious incompetence.

And those were days of utter delight for the open fields and dense thickets were heaven for us both. Sometimes, when we rested in a dry ditch with a January gale peeling our senses I would lecture him about the folly of his ways and I swear he would snicker and protest that, dammit, he was doing his best and what more could a master require?

Our dog Sam features in page after page of my game register which records my shooting days in detail and if I quote from my entry for 1st February 1982 perhaps you will understand the more fully the weird relationship between this master and his canine clown: "Last day of another shooting season and late afternoon I take Sam for what I know must be his very final day in the woods. The old fool is as excited and keen as ten years ago though his rheumatism means he will never hunt with me again. In the gloaming I shoot a high cock pheasant over the big ditch and Sam swims across and retrieves it from the plough. But he refuses to swim back and in the dark I am required to wade through the icy water and carry dog and cock back to the wood. I pray nobody is watching this madness though as I haul him up the slippery bank I am crying with laughter."

That night I massaged his old legs and carried him upstairs to his bed on the landing where he slept the sleep of a retired warrior and, doubtless, dreamed of his last wild pheasant.

Our dog Sam sat daily at my feet under the big old partners' desk at which I have scribbled these many years. He followed me round the house, into the garden, up the village street with an endless devotion.

But he was not just a one-man dog; he was the family dog and would behave with the same inane incorrigibility with my wife and children as with me.

He was, I suppose, the very cement in the fabric of our close family life for he lived through the 14 most important years of our growing children and aided them in their long struggle towards adulthood.

He was omnipresent for he was never absent and went with us

on family holidays. Indeed, he swam in most of our coastal waters and wantonly destroyed sand castles built by other families on the sands of Norfolk, the Gower and the West Country.

Our dog Sam lies in the grave I dug for him. It seemed right that I should be with him at the end and somehow that simple burial became the last link in that chain of inexplicable loyalty which is the chief glory of a man's relationship with his dog.

Gardens and Countryside

THE MOLE'S REVENGE

The common mole - or Talpa europoea as you would call him - has always left our garden alone. We have never suffered from mole hills and the reason I suspect, is that the mole is at heart a kindly soul and whenever he surfaces and pokes his head through the moss on our lawns he says to himself: "Cor, what a shambles! This bloke has quite enough trouble without us piling any more on". And off he scurries in search of a proper lawn with real grass where he can bring tears to the eyes of the gardener.

Therefore I have long regarded this little insectivorous mammal with something akin to affection and my fondness for him increased in large lumps this week when I heard how he became, albeit unwittingly, the means of providing an old chum of mine with the chance to Get His Own Back.

Step forward, please, Old Chum, Mr Colin Everett, a former member of the Cambridgeshire constabulary, who has resided these several years in Rectory Farm Road, Little Wilbraham.

No doubt many of you will know him well for not only is he a most gregarious gentleman but he was also a traffic policeman and if you met him in that latter guise then serve you right.

Now living next door to Our Chum in that charming hamlet is, oddly enough, a gentleman by the name of Ian Everitt and though their names differ by one letter their sense of humour runs along parallel lines.

For when Master Everett went away for a weekend some little time ago Master Everitt "borrowed" a "For Sale" sign, stuck it in Master Everett's garden and sat back and watched the ensuing chaos with no little amusement.

Colin vowed vengeance. No matter how long it takes, he warned Ian, I will have you. The threat hung in the air for some time and Ian relaxed. Then he discovered, to his profound horror for he is the keenest of gardeners, signs of a wandering mole on his patch. He was about to go on holiday. What was to be done, he asked his neighbour? Our kind Old Chum bade him take his holiday with confidence. He would catch the mole and ensure that Ian's garden would remain chaste and cleansed of roaming moles.

Imagine, therefore, the shock which was to greet Ian upon his return from distant parts when he found exactly 14 mole hills dotted about his formely immaculate lawn. Imagine, therefore, his surprise when, in a fury and a panic, he rushed out, cases still packed, to dig away until he found the tunnel and thereafter the offending mole.

Imagine, therefore, his astonishment after removing several mole hills at not being able to find so much as a single hole under them.

Yes, gentle reader, you are right in one. No sooner had M Everitt set off on his hols than Our Chum nipped over the wall into the churchyard where moles proliferate, gathered a sackful of mole hills and carefully rearranged 'em.......

Glorious, therefore, is the jolly jape. But remember: heaven awards the vengeance due!

A GOOD OLD 'UN

There is at the far end of our orchard an apple tree of great age. It is gnarled, twisted, decrepit. It is ill-kempt, uncared-for, ravaged by time and neglect. Its body is but a shell and ivy seeks to strangle it. It has absolutely nothing going for it and doubtless, it is the butt of all the younger, more elegant and comely trees elsewhere in the orchard, spurned and scorned by them on account of its ugliness.

And yet......it remains my favourite tree of them all for each year at this lovely time when the long tailed pheasants cough and croak over the orchard wall and soft mists shroud each dawn, that old tree comes into its own and shows up its younger arboreal colleagues for the strutting peacocks they really are. You see, each year it produces a luscious harvest of the very finest blushing cookers you ever did see. It shrugs off its weariness and transmutes itself into a cornucopia brimming with fine apples.

Whence comes its annual display of strength I know not. Nor do I care and I choose to leave the old tree as it is for two very good reasons. Firstly, without any help, encouragement or guidance it throws off enough fruit every autumn to keep us in apple tuffees, apple crumbles, apple tarts, and apple pies until well into the next year.

Secondly, and more importantly, every year it fills me with hope. For we have much in common that old tree and me (please re-read paragraph one to understand what I mean) and when I'm high up the ladder among its tired branches garnering its proud harvest I always allow myself a small smile. You see, like me that tree knows a trick or two that the youngsters don't. It has also learned, as I have, that it takes a good old 'un to beat a good young 'un.

SHADOW OF A PERIWINKLE

We open today's proceedings, m'Lud, with the appearance of two men in the dock and we'll start if it so pleases you with Mr Jack Ayers of the village of Lode who is guilty beyond the shadow of a periwinkle of filling my wife with false hope and a sense of unwarranted vanity.

The facts, my Lord, are these: of late that wife of mine has been wandering about wearing the smug smile of a moggy which has just fallen into a lake of double cream. So disturbed was I by this strange departure from her usual mien that I caused extensive inquiries to be made. Seems she was over at Anglesey Abbey just down the road from us the other day and there she bumped into the accused Mr Jack Ayers who, as you know, is brother of the great and now retired head gardener at the Abbey, Mr Noel Ayers. Now Jack did not recognise my wife when she spoke to him and she introduced herself as "Janet Jeacock". The accused looked at her and said: "Ah, you must be Michael Jeacock's daughter". She is purring still, my Lord, and I urge you to find him guilty as charged.

Then we turn to Mr Harold Preston of the City of Ely a man who is known widely in that handsome place despite the fact, m'Lud, that he has hidden for many years behind the alias of "Sunny". He spends much of his time in the company of other undesirables in a hostelry in Ely in which I, too, find myself upon occasion, called the "High Flyer". I intend to prove to you, m'Lud, that he is guilty of using his own low, cunning wiles to satisfy his apparently insatiable demand for a form of brown ale which that hostelry provides for its denizens and the evidence is as follows:

Beyond the car park of the "Flyer" lies a large vegetable garden which, it must be admitted, is beautifully maintained by the accused himself and therein are to be found most excellent examples of the plantsman's art, in particular, several rows of carrots.

During my visit last week, m'Lud, I happened to glance over the garden fence and to congratulate the accused upon the healthy appearance of his carrots and he forthwith offered me a bait of them to take with me upon my journey. Although I noticed a faint smile playing around the rubicund gentleman's lips I accepted the handful of carrots with my accustomed grace and without fear of harmful consequence. Upon offering him reimbursement in the form of coin of the realm for his labours and kindness he refused to accept any payment saying with a clarity which still rings in my ears: "That's okay, guvnor, I'll just have a pint when we get into the pub."

And when I walked into the bar, m'Lud, carrying my little handful of carrots, there was a roar of incredulous laughter and loud, coarse shouts of: "Cor! Sunny's found another one". And: "That Jeacock's as daft as he looks". And the regulars explained as I stood there bewildered. For what the villain had done was to get away once more with his favourite con-trick of giving away a tanner's worth of carrots in return for 90p worth of brown and mild.

As the landlord, Mr Bert Hearn, would have told you m'Lud had he been called to give evidence, those three short rows of carrots are worth about five thousand quid a year to Mr Sunny Preston and again I urge you to find him guilty as charged.

TAKING THE ROUGH WITH THE ROUGH

There exists within the British race a vein of awkwardness, a subculture even, which permits us to delight in adversity, to enjoy foul conditions and to smile into the teeth of the gale. It is why the Bank Holiday was invented.

The theory exploded upon me with vivid clarity on Monday afternoon as we huddled soaked and soggy inside a beer tent at the Fenland Country Fair. Outside there were stair-rods of rain but still the holidaymakers queued for hot taters at one stall, ice cream at another and mushy peas over at Mrs Greenhill's noshery.

Under the canvas of our tent there was huge merriment of a variety which it is impossible to find in the warmth of the Mediterranean sun; rain trickled down the inside of our Barbours, Melvyn Ginn's terrier dug frantically in search of a non-existent rat and folk giggled as they tripped over his lead. Black labradors with velvety coats eyed each other with lustful glances - as indeed, did some of their owners - and as the weather grew even more horrible so the joyousness of the occasion increased. The turf beneath our feet became a squelchy quagmire, the tales of exploits with gun, rod and hound became more outrageous and as the downpour became a deluge so jollity outmanoeuvred and conquered the inhospitable elements and we all thumbed our noses at the grumpy weatherman, spat in the eye of another lousy Bank Holiday Monday and ordered some more beer.

Mind there's nowt wrong with the occasional touch of the broiling sun although I've always believed that any fool of a nation can live in constant heat while for our up-and-down climate there is a requirement for a type of mad genius which is peculiar to the Brits. There was certainly nothing amiss with the sun which shone down upon the fair city of Ely on Saturday where herself and I found ourselves as guests of the Ely and District Horticultural Society at their 59th annual show. They had very kindly invited me to declare the show open under the mistaken impression that I know something about gardening, an impression fostered, mayhap, by the endless series of outright lies and multiple falsehoods which I have promulgated in these columns over the years and which I assumed nobody believed. But they're a kind and trusting lot over in Ely which is why we spent Saturday afternoon looking with bemused astonishment at flowers and vegetables which, compared to mine, came from another planet.

There was, however, a touch of sadness to the afternoon for the good gardeners of Ely told me that, as with so many other facets of our national life, the youngsters are "not coming along" as they should be. As the old 'uns drop off the perch and allotments become available they are no longer snatched up by youngsters anxious to delight in the tilling of the soil.

Which is a considerable shame because the pleasure and sense of fulfilment to be found in gardening are not lightly to be ignored. There is not just the joy of eating one's own vegetables, of sniffing one's own flowers; there are other, less obvious charms. Like being able to escape from the missus for an hour or two. One friend keeps a bottle of scotch in one of his wellies in his greenhouse and spends many a happy hour alone in there, un-nagged and at peace with himself. I know some other chaps who have taken allotments (I will refrain from divulging their whereabouts in Cambridge) where they gather together on Saturdays for long games of cribbage in one the sheds there. They buy vegetables on the way home.

So come on you youngsters. get stuck in. You might even get round to enjoying the gardening itself.

"MORNING, LEEKS"

Percy Blinco always brings about the offical ending of summer so far as I am concerned and I thank him for it. You see, although the harvest is not yet in, although there is still a burning sun and although the raspberries still sit lushly on the bending bough, I always turn my thoughts to winter when, as I have just so done, I stick Percy's magnificent leek plants into their watery holes.

The leek is our winter mainstay and even though the sweat drips from what was once a forelock as I plant 'em out, the mind looks forward to the winter table heavy with roast pheasant and leek, rabbit pie and leek, jugged hare and leek, orangey mallard and leek.

I tend to boast somewhat about the leeks for they are out of the ordinary but the truth is that I am indebted to Percy who always supplies me with plants which are very nearly big enough to eat now. But one thing has puzzled me for years. How is it that, though Percy's leeks start off the same size as mine, his always end up twice the size of mine come the winter? I reckon it's the way he speaks to them.

HELP!!!

That percipient old codger Kipling decreed that "the Glory of the Garden glorifieth everyone" and whilst I have no desire to argue with him I do sometimes wish that those who find themselves so glorified would muck in and help occasionally.

In other words, if you find yourselves wandering down our village street don't suspect for a moment that I will be in any way offended should you decide to pop in to do an hour's weeding, a few spits of digging and a bit of hoeing and trimming.

For the truth is that a garden, especially one the size of ours, is a demanding mistress and there are brief moments during the gardening year when the ancient cranium finds itself stuffed with doubts about the wisdom of ever becoming involved with Mother Soil.

But then, on a morning like this (it's Monday. It's warm and still; there is bird-song and there is plenty scattered o'er a smiling land) it all becomes worthwhile for rarely in all the years I have toiled, fumed, gloated, cursed and exulted in the garden have I ever known such prodigious and satisfying growth as I witnessed a few minutes ago from our back door.

I counted with some smugness more than 30 different vegetables and soft fruits in the kitchen garden, some weary with weight, others rampant with youthful energy. It was a sight designed to remove from the memory the aching back and the sweating brow.

However, let's return to Kipling and I urge upon all my relations, friends and passers-by, the strength of his argument in these lines:

"There's not a pair of legs so thin, there's not a head so thick,
There's not a hand so weak and white, nor yet a heart so sick
But it can find some needful job that's crying to be done,
For the Glory of the Garden glorifieth everyone."

FLAMING MOSS

"Spring ain't yet sprung, mate
And the grass ain't hardly riz;
But one thing's sartin sure, mate:
Our flamin' mossiz."

I place before you with modest pride my contribution to the new Cambridge University Golden Treasury of Important Modern Verse which I penned following twin incidents over last weekend.

Firstly, on Saturday - you may recall that we actually enjoyed several hours of startling sunshine - I put our mower through the acre or so of greenery which surrounds our home and I dare swear before an honest attorney that the wretched machine dragged less than a score of wispy blades of grass into its capable maw.

Yet I was forced to empty stone after stone of verdant mosses onto our now mountainous cuttings heap. (There are, to be fair, several large patches of celandine, buttercup, daisy and assorted thistles which have managed to burst through the cloying stranglehold of our lake of moss).

There is little point in recommending moss killer or grass inducer. I know when I'm beaten.

Then, secondly, on Sunday herself and I popped down the road to our friendly next-door neighbour, Lord Fairhaven, a description, I should say, which I normally reserve to impress visitors from the United States of A, but since they don't seem so keen on flying here any more I though I might as well waste it on you lot out there.

However, that aside, we toddled off to Anglesey Abbey to have a quick gander at the magnificent hyacinth garden which is currently in full and glorious bloom. Four thousand plants, just blue and white, in a perfection of symmetry; same height, perfect lines, immaculate, a total contrast to the wonderful chaos of less-disciplined spring flowers - exuberant daffs, wandering snowdrops and dash-about-anywhere aconites.

No. The hyacinth garden is the Guards Brigade on parade compared with the Band of Hope after a night on the whacky-baccy.

But I digress. For what really upset me at Anglesey Abbey were those blasted lawns. Acre upon acre of weedless grass. Hectares of billiard tables. Green as grass, if you know what I mean. And the moss? I very much doubt if his lordship and the National Trust would so much recognise the name, ne'er mind the substance.

Then I reckon that their head gardener Richard Ayers should know a thing or two after 25 years at the Abbey but I remind him of the words of that other great poet Robert Browning: "What's come to perfection perishes. Things learned on earth we shall practise in heaven. Work done least rapidly, Art most cherishes."

PASS BY, WORLD

So I'm striding out across the wet plough with Ron Greenhill on Saturday morning hoping to bag a brace of hedgerow pheasants for the pot when suddenly ten roe deer go prancing across the skyline at the top of our field, all in a perfect line and graceful as the most polished ballerinas.

The only sound is of half a gale moaning through the tall poplars behind us. Silently we watch the dainty deer disappear and we wish them safe journey and good luck through the coming winter.

A few yards further on and from the hedge which separates us rises a sparrow hawk with a gentle, floating majesty. We watch the raptor soar away and we bid him good hunting.

Chippenham village is merely a mile off but our English countryside has organised itself so delicately over the past two hundred years that it is possible to slip out of civilisation with a few long strides and those of us who are able, or who choose to seek the escape, are the lucky ones, for the sight of those lovely deer and that daring hawk will lodge in our memories for years, long after the thrills of urban society are forgotten.

I mention this because last week a report out from some national body or other showed that two thirds of the folk in this kingdom of ours only use the countryside to pass through it on their way from home to work and when I first read this I was horrified.

However, not only am I President of the National Society of Cowards but I'm also Chairman of NASB - the National Association of Selfish, er, Blighters. And on second thoughts I welcomed the news for though those two thirds of the nation know not what they are missing, equally there is no doubt that if they were all to start rushing around the countryside then Ron, me, the deer and the hawk would find ourselves submerged 'neath an untidy tide of humans and bang would go the delights of solitude. So keep driving by, folks, and leave us in peace.

With Gun and Ferret

MONSTER OF SIX MILE BOTTOM

Forced myself to engage upon a dose of autumn digging in ye garden on Sunday by which I mean that I started on Sunday to catch up with the digging I was too idle to do last autumn. Anyway, the upshot of all the exercise was that by eventide the brow was definitely puckered, the sedge undoubtedly withered and the throat was as dry as the epicentre of the Gobi desert in mid-drought. So I adjourned to the "Wheatsheaf" at Stow-cum-Quy, a hostelry infested by sundry countryfolk and sportsmen with whom it is pleasant to relax and who are always good for a natter about rustic happenings.

Which is how I came to be introduced to what must be one of the largest of wild rabbits ever seen in the kingdom and that, I hasten to assure you, was before I had even sipped a soupcon of the amber nectar.

It came about thus: next door to the Wheatsheaf lives David Roff, keeper on the Quy Hall estate. And in his deep freeze he has this remarkable rabbit shot recently by his colleague Martin Taylor over at the Six Mile Bottom estate. Martin was so astonished when he picked up the rabbit that he asked David to have it stuffed and mounted so that he can win bets about its size during the rest of his days.

For the rabbit is just one ounce short of weighing seven and a half pounds. Now if you don't know much about brer rabbit I should point out that the average weight of the wild bunny is between two and half and three and a half pounds. And seven and a half pounds is the normal weight of a hare. But before you start saying - ah, well, it must have been a cross with a hare, I should again point out that such a cross is genetically impossible and that the hybrid simply does not exist.

I hear you say that maybe it was a heavily pregnant rabbit. Well, if it was that's the second miracle for this beast was a buck and not even an old one for an examination of its teeth showed no sign of advancing years. And just to make sure I wasn't dreaming I took with me from the pub into David's cosy and delightful cottage Mr Malcolm Hall of Swaffham Prior who happened to be in the watering hole with me. He's bowled over thousands of rabbits in his time and he was just as astonished at the beast's size as yours truly.

I'm left now with the following thoughts: what caused this phenomenon? Are there any records of similarly huge rabbits, or even bigger ones? And how massive would that old rabbit have looked to Master Hall and me if we'd had a jar or two before examining it?

In matters of shooting I have always agreed with the late President Roosevelt who declared: "Laying stress upon the mere quantity of game killed and the publication of the record of slaughter are sure signs of unhealthy decadence in sportsmanship", and the real field sportsman will always prefer quality which yields a sufficiency for the pot. 'Twas not always so and in the bad old days of the grande battue there were some incredibly bizarre performances. The largest bag of rabbits shot in one day, for example, was at Blenheim in Oxfordshire in 1898 when five guns killed a total of 6,943. The guns were the Duke of Marlborough, Prince Victor Duleep Singh, Prince Frederick Duleep Singh, Sir Robert Gresley and Mr Robert Wombwell (was the latter, I wonder, any relation to the vast tribe of Cambridgeshire Wombwells?). They shot from 9.10am to 5.40pm allowing 35 minutes for luncheon and though that form of madness is now long gone, one is still bemused as to why they should have desired to do it and how they managed it physically. Mind you, that was as nothing to the exploits of the Marquis of Ripon (he was so fast with the gun he could kill 28 birds in a minute) whose game records show that between 1867 and 1923 his tally was exactly 500,256 head of different game of which 34,118 were rabbits.

But I'll bet half a crown and my old shut-knife to a piece of binder twine that he never saw one as big as the Monster of Six Mile Bottom .....

CROWN COCK-BIRD

I found myself standing alone, in an old wood on an ancient estate on the south Derbyshire-Staffordshire border. Torrential rain and tree-bowing storms had abated and there was a strange, deep calm in the clearing where I stood under an oak tree waiting for the pheasants to appear. A placid but clear stream ambled past me through brambled and nettly banks. Two raucous jays flip-flapped about in the roofs of tall trees. Leaves which had been royally gold a week earlier were now common and dully brown and plopped with little dignity into the water. Suddenly, upstream, my eye was taken by a flash of brilliant blue. A kingfisher came hurtling towards me, zig-zagging along the meandering course of the stream. It flashed in and out of my life in three bats of the eyelid and I was grateful. A grey heron rose from its sentry-like position under the lee of the bank and sloped off in ponderous flight after the kingfisher. An elephant following a gazelle.

I had pinched a day off work to shoot with friends on that old estate, the Big House of which is now owned by the Home Office and is used as a Detention Centre for young offenders. One pheasant killed by a gun on my right fell into the prison compound behind the high, barbed wire fence. A blue-boiler-suited inmate strolled over and picked up the cock bird. "Chuck it over, please", said the gun. The young man on the other side of the fence used a phrase which, I suspect, is not in common usage at High Table in Trinity College. Then, announcing that the bird was now Crown Property, he marched away with it. That lad will undoubtedly go far.

FERDINAND THE FEROCIOUS

Normally when I take our two ferrets out for a gentle stroll I do so with a smile upon my fizzog for we get on well as a threesome. They scuttle along making happy twittering noises though I do occasionally have a problem with one of them - Ferdinand the Ferocious - for he is an indolent chap and likes to climb up my trouser leg (on the outside, madam) and to cling there hitching a lift.

If there is nobody around I enjoy nattering to them and I swear that once when I promised 'em a day's rabbiting they uttered squeals of delight though it may well have been that I accidentally trod on one of them.

But when we were scuffling through the leaves together the other sun-bright morn I felt obliged to tell them in sombre terms of the dangers facing country sports in this neck of the fens because, believe it or not, once again Cambridgeshire County Councillors are being forced into wasting their precious time by debating the pros and cons of hunting. For the umpteenth time Labour members of the council are seeking the banning of hunting on council-owned farmland in the county despite having been defeated so often in this continuing, acrimonious battle.

I do believe that Fred and Ferdie were dismayed at this news for, naturally, they are on the side of the sportsmen since hunting is in their very blood. Indeed, ferreting is the most basic kind of hunting and for many just as thrilling as the pink-coated variety though somewhat less expensive.

Anyway, I told the two chaps that, yes, the anti-hunting brigade were at it again which is a great pity for without doubt the whole campaign is a mixture of political expediency and a misguided desire to promote animal welfare. I reminded my two little mates that many anti-hunting Socialists had conveniently forgotten that the last major government inquiry into hunting, the Scott Henderson Committee, had, in fact, been set up under a Labour government. And that investigation which looked in depth at the alternatives which would replace hunting, showed that abolition would in no way benefit the animals concerned.

I mentioned to the ferrets side issues involved in the argument, such as individual freedom to participate in a legal sport, the huge loss of jobs which abolition would lead to - farriers, kennelmen, grooms, saddlers, hay merchants etc etc - a traditional pattern of country life destroyed. Then I read out to them a quotation from the well-known London barrister Ann Mallalieu who is both a paid-up member of the Labour Party and of the British Fields Sports Society who said recently after pointing out alternative forms of fox control: "A vote against hunting is a vote to increase animal suffering".

Hunting, of course, is a vastly emotive subject and I know that what I have just written will bring forth a plenitude of letters from well-meaning readers, a handful of cranks and no end of folk who, though filled with good intentions, know as much about the fox and the hunting of it as I know about the internal combustion engine. No complaints about the letters because we're all entitled to express our opinions. But before I'm attacked for hunting the fox let me tell you that I do not ride to hounds. But let me add immediately that the only reason I do not do so is because they haven't invented a horse big enough to carry me.

HER DIADEM A CLOUDLESS SKY

I played hell last week in this column because the fen had been so inhospitable to us when we were out cock-shooting. Foul and dank she was and wearing, as I said then, the make-up of an idle slut. I threatened to address her with some severity if she did not change her mood on the final day of the shooting season which fell last Saturday. She read the piece, obviously, for you will recall that Saturday was probably the loveliest day of the winter - this or any other. That distant fen was dowdy no more. She tricked herself out in the rich raiment of a proud princess. Her diadem was a cloudless sky, her pendant a gleaming sun. The black fen soil was her gown embroidered with a million sparkling diamonds of frost. The icy dykes were her Cinderella's slippers of pure glass. The crisp air was her offering of champagne and when, at the day's end, she bade us farewell, the sunken sun had clothed her in a cerise ball-gown.

Fanciful? Well, maybe. But that's how I saw her on Saturday and that's how I'll always remember her.

THINNING OUT THE CLAYS

Back to the countryside and on to a landed gentleman who lives not a million miles from my own home. He is a courtly squire, good-humoured and generous. But, like the rest of us, occasionally he gets things slightly wrong.

As in the case of the local lads who spend their Sunday mornings clay pigeon shooting. The Major, as we shall call him, offered the chaps a piece of his land where they could blast away to their barrels' content and so they did. And, after a year of sport they decided to give him a bottle of scotch as a token of their appreciation. They presented it to him at the Hall and were somewhat puzzled when he asked them how many they had shot. Several thousands, replied one of the clay shooters. "Excellent", said the Major, "the blighters needed thinning out".

A PREGNANT FAIRY?

There is little respect these days for the decrepit and the ridiculous as I discovered after collecting some cartridges from Gallyons in Cambridge before setting off for pheasant land.

Dressed properly in my plus-twos, cut to the knee, with stout, long woollen stockings below, I paused to watch the antics of a group of youths with dyed Mohican hair and gaudy clothing. I smiled indulgently at their ludicrous attire. One pointed across the road and they began to laugh - at me. One shouted: "It's a pregnant fairy with boots on"; another: "It's a potato with two matches stuck in it." I shot them a glance of withering scorn and left them doubled up with laughter on the footpath.

OLD LARRY LEPUS

Exactly thirty years to the day after our Queen's good, brave and kindly father died at his beloved Sandringham following a hare shoot there I was walking across mile upon mile of plough accompanied by nearly 100 other armed men. We too, like the old King, were out under the wide East Anglian sky on an annual hare cull; not the finest of sporting activities but a necessary one if the crops are not to be trimmed by the equivalent of flocks of hungry sheep. To the townie who only sees 'they old hayers' when, in the madness of March, they stand up to box each other, our fields look bare and lifeless now but, in fact, they are teeming with those rodent mammals of little courage and less cunning but whose 28 teeth will nibble through growing produce with the swiftness of a taxman attacking a pay packet. But it was more the robust men taking part in the long march through three parishes, over dyke and ditch and across breath-jerking soft plough and welcoming, easily walked stubble, who interested me the most. A motley cross section of blokes with here a tall Old-Etonian bearing a turn-of-the-century Purdey 12-bore of exquisite workmanship and there a dark-skinned Fen tiger from the inner-most wilds of what I still call Huntingdonshire. He was carrying an ancient hammer gun, worth perhaps a thousandth of the aristocratic Purdey yet both guns did their deadly work in similar fashion. The dark one, a single gold earring nestling beneath his curling black hair, was a man of the open spaces. He told me how he had tried factory work twice. But each time the soft spring breezes had stroked the fens he had chucked it and gone back to farm work, less well-paid but infinitely more rewarding. If ever he had to work inside again, he said, he thought he would turn his old gun on himself. Dotted throughout the fens are families of swarthy, silky-eyed folk like him and I suspect they stem from the Welsh drovers who, in yesteryear, brought sheep from the hills to be fattened on lush eastern pastures and who stayed on in the flatlands to bring a different sort of plumpness to our womenfolk.

We had two days with the hares and at the end of the second I sat with daft old Sam, the Worst Gundog in England, before a crackling fire and comforted him in his anguish at hearing the shooting and not being able to join in. I raised a glass to King George and thanked him for the selfless training he had handed down to the girl who became Queen and hoped that the manner of his going had been softened by his last hours with old Larry Lepus.

THE ENGLISH FURROW

To say that they don't make 'em any more like James Wentworth Day would be the understatement of the year. He has just died at the age of 83 and he was one of the last of the great field sportsmen spawned by the fens for although the newspaper obituaries claimed that he was an Essex man that was merely his adopted county and he was always immensely proud of being born in a thatched manor in Wicken, hard by the primeval fen in that Cambridgeshire village. He knew and loved his countryside and in his prolific writings he always bore in mind that in the hearts of most town-dwellers there lurks a latent villager. He could paint brilliant verbal pictures of the lonely places and of the animals and birds he came to know so well during a long life of sport and observation. Wentworth Day was born at a time when game shooting was at its pinnacle in this country and great shots abounded on their well-keepered partridge manors, their heavily stocked pheasant coverts and their unspoiled moors teeming with grouse. He would speak of men like Rimington-Wilson who, for forty summers, would swing along carrying an iron walking stick weighing seven pounds so that his arms were ready flexed for the August shooting; of Ivan Cobbold who regularly fired 30,000 cartridges in a season; and, of course, of Tom de Grey, sixth Lord Walsingham, greatest of all East Anglian shots. It was he who would travel over to Wicken wearing a cap made from the skin of a hedgehog, a snakeskin waistcoat and a moleskin jacket to shoot vast quantities of fenland snipe with Freddie Johnson of Wicken Hall and Wentworth Day's uncle, old Isaac Aspland and maybe Bill "Longbow" Howlett of Barton Mills. It was Walsingham, of course, who shot 1070 grouse with 1510 cartridges in one day, a feat which never has been and never will be repeated. Wentworth Day travelled the world in search of different quarries but his thoughts were always in that Old England he knew as a fenland boy and even as an old man his heart would leap up at the thought of grey geese coming calling off the tides or at the memory of the time he shot over Sandringham's broad acres with King George V. He believed mightily that strength of character springs from the sports of the field, that they are part of the very soul and spirit of the land and he once declared: "Sport will never die so long as a ploughshare turns an English furrow".

DRAT AND DOUBLE DRAT

Saturday, late afternoon. The sun has slunk off leaving a mauve sky slashed with pink. On the banks of a sluggish stream near Newmarket six men are crouched, hidden in dense bushes.

They are expectant and straining eyes and ears for the approach of their quarry - the night flight of ducks. This is to be the highlight of a day's shooting and silence and stillness are essential.

Slowly and with infinite care one of the guns stretches to relieve a cramped muscle. And just as slowly he loses his balance and topples over into the semi-stagnant water and slime.

He sinks in and thrashes wildly like a floundering and reluctant mollusc with his free left arm, for his right hand holds his shotgun clear of the stinking water, a latter-day Excalibur.

His cry of "I've fallen in" is greeted by the gun on his left, one Malcolm Hall, with the reply: "Yes, we can all hear you. Shut up - you'll frighten the duck".

Neither parade ground nor football terrace can match the invective which issues from the still-floundering fool in the stream and his suggestion as to what should be done with and to the approaching ducks are, upon reflection, unreasonable, unjust and, considering the height at which they are flying, physically impossible.

Finally, still inventing incredibly vivid phrases, he emerges unaided from the stream, the dark sky rent by hideous peals of laughter from his fellows. The duck are disappearing in ever-widening circles for more peaceful parts of the firmament.

It is a long and uncomfortable drive home and when I reach it I am greeted by herself with: "Don't think you're coming in here covered in mud".

For, dear reader, 'twas your humble servant who was dunked. And if you don't believe me ask the aforementioned Master Hall of Swaffham Prior, John Dawson of the same village, George Weir of Longmeadow, Ron Greenhill of Reach and farmer David Butler of Stow-cum-Quy whose duck-shooting I ruined. And ask the poor souls at The Swiss Laundry in Cherryhinton Road, Cambridge, who are still trying to scrape the mud from my clothes.

"COCK OVER"

On our day with the gun we found ourselves in a marshy wood over near Fordham and within minutes we had seen bounding deer, flittering snipe, cunning partridges, lolloping hares, swirling pigeons, skittish rabbits and hurtling pheasants. Plus, I'm happy to say, dancing woodcock.

The woodcock must have been home-bred for I believe it to be too early for the migratory variety to have arrived so far inland. A beautiful bird, the woodcock, but perhaps the most dangerou of all in the shooting field for its uneven manner of flight and its propensity for flying head high along the line of guns leads to many a nasty accident.

Thus, when the ancient gamekeeper was asked how he accounted for his living to 100 he replied: "By taking a bottle of whisky a day and by throwing myself flat on my face whenever I heard the shout 'woodcock'!"

BREATH LIKE POWDER PUFFS

Then, on Saturday after the finest day's pheasant shooting in memory, we are standing in the parkland of Hengrave Hall in Suffolk awaiting the final drive. The sun is almost finished for the day and the stillness is only broken by the tap-tapping of the beaters' sticks.

The hollows of that ancient park fill slowly with afternoon mist, silvery and haunting. Down at the end of the avenue of cedars the Elizabethan Hall, somnolent in its aristocratic repose, becomes engulfed in the advancing gloom and suddenly, from a round wood, deer bound, startled and elegant in full flight.

They scatter over the park, their breath hanging like powder puffs on the air behind them, and finally they melt into the mist and are gone. For a few moments we were returned to a golden age and our century had vanished as surely as the deer.

THE HALF DUCK

Let me tell you two plain tales which will illustrate the deep divide between the preposterous folly of youth and the sane reason of middle-age.

We begin with my son and heir who recently finds himself heavy with cold, feverish of brow and aching of eye. Reasonably, he decides upon an early night and, since the morrow is a Sunday, perhaps a morning in bed will help to repel the dreaded lurgy.

Comes the morn and with it an early phone call from his chum Andrew Greenhill of Reach. He knows where there are grey battalions of wood pigeon drawn up and would Simon like to grab his gun so that they might sally forth into the ice and snow to do battle? Never was an illness flung aside with more disdain. A quick breakfast and off to a distant field of lucerne. Herself and I exchanged glances.

Ah, said I, the incredible impetuosity of youth! The imprudence, the foolhardy precipitancy of the young! Thus, quoth she, did incautious Hotspur go forth. And serve him right, said I, if the dozy twerp gets pneumonia.

Whereas, you see, a few days later I am stricken with a similar bug and as I stagger from the breakfast table I build myself a mountainous fire of apple and plum logs before which I sit warm but glum as I watch the snowflakes curl in the wind.

A phone call comes for me from Malcolm Hall of Swaffham Prior. He knows where there are teal and snipe. And maybe a hare or two.

I look at the blazing logs and at the half blizzard outside. After half a century, discrimination becomes a man and prudence is all-embracing. Sagacious rationality comes with middle-age and judgement is unwarped by urgent desire.

Yes, well. So I put on my green wellies, unsheath my twelve-bore and step out into the winter's wild lament with a sore head but with a singing heart. I think herself said something about no fool like an old fool but I never really wanted to grow up anyway.

Thus it came to pass that we had teal for lunch on Sunday (indeed, we also had mallard, pheasant and snipe) but it was the teal we enjoyed most. It's the smallest of indigenous British ducks and many would reckon it the tastiest. It is still known in the fens as a "half duck", not because of its size but because its marketable value has always been about half that of the Wild Duck or mallard.

By the way, the female teal is a terrible tease and during her courtship time she will allow several males to vie with each other in friendly competition for her favours. It is all rather human-like for while the drakes are showing off to her they will occasionally give a low, double whistle of the variety to be heard on many a street corner. But, unlike a lot of humans, once teal have paired off they become strictly monogamous.

They're also fiercely protective of their young and there is the story of the lad working on Lord Cavan's estate in Achill who found a brood of downy nestlings and drove them before him back to the farm. The mother teal followed in great distress ignoring other people on the way and when the boy finally drove the brood into a shed the mother continued to follow and thus sacrificed herself to captivity to be with her young.

The English Pub

BLIND BOB'S PUB

So I'm standing at the bar of the Royal Oak wondering how I can con my old chum Alan Burns into buying me another half pint of the landlord's malted nectar when in walks this pleasant-looking youth from the one-armed bandit firm. He empties the wretched machine and is about to count the glinting piles of florins he's extracted when the phone rings in the recesses of the kitchen. It's an urgent call for him from his firm. But the lad, on his first visit to the Oak, eyes the only two customers present - the aforementioned Burns and yours truly - and announces firmly to landlord Bob Scrutton: "I'm not leaving this money unguarded. It's more than my job's worth". Oh-ho, says I. Charming. For although a good argument could be made that I have the appearance of a seedily itinerant Mexican banker on the lookout for a spare peso or three, Master Burns is patently an honest burgher, a citizen of obvious rectitude albeit reluctant to buy two half pints on the trot. But before hostilities can break out landlord Scrutton declaims in a calming and assuring voice: "Worry not, young man, for I will keep a close eye on the spondulicks pending your return." Whereupon the lad is comforted and goes into the hinterland of the pub to speak with his masters and although the three of us laugh until we nearly spill our beer we haven't the heart to tell him when he comes back that the guardian of his treasure is the only blind publican in the whole of the kingdom.

SCUTTLE THE DOMINOES

There is a certain pinstriped prune, a silly city slicker, a wearisome wally who had best keep his daft self out of East Anglia unless he has an urgent desire to be garrotted or belted with the nearest futtock.

I shall not name him lest the mob rise up and seek him in his London lair and there put him to the sword. Suffice it to say that he runs an outfit up in the metropolis which advises brewers on how to turn perfectly good and honest hostelries into what he calls "fun pubs".

And in an interview in one of the papers the other day he made a statement which left me stuttering and speechless, rigid with horror and shaking with fury, whey-faced with fear and purple with indignation - all at the same time - and even now I hesitate to repeat it in case I cause a public mischief.

He said, I'm sorry to say, that it was his company's intention TO DO AWAY WITH THE SPIT AND SAWDUST TYPE OF ENGLISH PUB.

Their plans, apparently, are to replace the traditional English boozer with "theme pubs", filled with noise and colour and packed with wives and kids and all that sort of rot.

I was having breakfast at the time that I read the report and I was so shattered and taken aback that I almost left my third banger. Herself is accustomed to my odd outbursts but even she was alarmed at my instant reaction.

"Why doesn't the fool go the whole hog and burn the dartboards and scuttle the domino tables?", I screamed. She, poor lass, was unaware of the cause of my apoplexy, and edged nervously towards the back door. "Why doesn't he chop up the shove ha'penny boards, rip out the bowling alleys, smash the pint tankards, abolish the cribbage leagues?", I bellowed.

Her ladyship finally discovered the reason for my upset and sought to soothe me with honeyed words. "Fear not", quoth she, "that sort of thing cannot happen in Old England."

"Can it not", hissed I. "If those flaming brewers thought they might squeeze another shekel out of the poor, beleaguered public by flogging their grannies they'd do so."

And with that I went off to Ely to declare open the new lavatories in a real pub in that fine and ancient city.

THE LOO OPENER

I confess that I am something of a newcomer to the art of offically opening loos but I performed this particular operation flushed with enthusiasm because I had heard wondrous tales of the marvellous beer which John Champion serves in his pub, the Prince Albert in Silver Street, Ely, and when he requested my presence to cut the, er, tape (it came off the sort of roll which small puppies chase on the telly), I felt it would be churlish to demur despite my inexperience.

So I took her herself with me - I like her to be at my side when I'm involved in important and pompous public occasions - and a rattling good time we had in that grand pub filled with laughter and good cheer, excellent grub and fine beer to say nowt of two of the smartest lavatories in the kingdom.

And on our way back through the fens it struck me forcibly that "fun" and "pub" are two three-lettered words which are synonymous and that it is quite superfluous to prefix "pub" with "fun". And, wappy city gent, you can keep your wandering hands off proper pubs like the Prince Albert.

AN AXE - LOST AND FOUND

Anyway, there we are, standing in the Oak on Saturday lunchtime watching Ben Blaydon's Jack Russell lapping up his master's Guinness while his back is turned - actually the little devil is quite content to slurp away at a pint of bitter as Stan Parsons knows to his cost - when in walks young Alex Kirby from Swaffham Prior.

"Identify that", he says, slipping a solid, newspaper-wrapped object into my hand. It is a piece of stone picked from a potato-sorting operation by his sister-in-law Mrs Tina Smith of Cambridge. Obviously it is a very fine and extremely ancient axe-head. It turned up, apparently, in a field near Wicken Fen on the edge of Soham Mere and it had lain there for a longish time for the Museum of Archaeology and Anthropology in Cambridge reckon it is a polished Neolithic axe-head some 5,000 years old.

Unused - its finely honed edge cuts newspaper like a razor - it would seem that its unlucky owner must have lost it before he could start chopping away at his kindling wood. Had the poor bloke lost it as it hurtled off the haft and plopped into deep fen water? And if so, what sort of curses did Neolithic man use in such a situation? The stone, said the museum, originated from Langdale in the Lake District. By what means and by what route of barter did that beautiful artefact reach the settlers in the fens?

Such questions filled our minds as we handled the perfectly proportioned axe in silence and almost with reverence for it is an object of almost magical delight.

So we went off home for lunch, wondering, some of us, if perhaps we might have been related to that unlucky, cursing, furious prehistoric man who never had a chance to use what must have been his proudest possession.

RANALD SPENDS 46p

We are a deeply divided community and it is all because our local worker in wood, Mr Ranald Scott, committed an act utterly out of character and so astonishing as to be worthy of public and permanent record.

You see, Ranald went out and spent some money.

Ranald, you understand, is an immigrant, a fugitive who fled from his lairdly Scottish background to seek his fortune in the soft terrain of Cambridgeshire. (Actually he discovered the delights of Greene King bitter at an early age and decided to remain within easy reach of the nectar).

He retains not only his charming Scottish burr but also the well-known and traditional Scottish habit of extreme prudence whereby he does not permit himself to pay tuppence if he can get away with paying nowt.

So you might imagine our surprise when he arrived at the Royal Oak t'other evening towing on a piece of red string an extremely happy-looking mongrel pup. He then announced: "Look what I've just bought".

The stunned silence which followed this remark was due not just to the fact that he had actually parted with money for a purpose other than to quench his own thirst but that he had actually spent it on something which would require further financial expenditure, for even a common cur has to be fed.

It seems that Ranald acquired the strange beast - its colours and shape defy rational analysis - for precisely 46p from a lad in Burwell; that odd sum having been arrived at because that was all the cash Ranald had on him at the time of the deal.

But what is causing us some concern is the fact that Ranald seems determined to dub the dog "Rover" because, he argues, nobody ever really calls a dog by that name outside of children's comics.

Half the lads in the Oak are in favour while the rest of us reckon that's just too easy, for a good name is better than precious ointment and for a hound of such undecipherable parentage a very special cognomen is required.

Therefore Ranald - he won't know this until he opens his Town crier - will send his cheque for another 46p to the reader who gives me the best suggestion for a name for this splendidly different pooch.

BIG 'TATERS, BIG MOUTH

They were talking in the Oak the other night about the bloke over in Suffolk who was lifting his main crop potatoes when the village bore looked over the garden fence and sneered at the small size of the taters. The gardener riposted without looking up: "Don't you worry, son. I grew 'em to fit my mouth, not yours".

SAME NAME

Then we got around to talking about gundogs and how odd it was that no matter what the beasts are named on their pedigrees, no matter by what names they may be called in the bosom of the family, they all end up with the same name shouted at them by their irate masters once they misbehave in the field. It's always roughly the same whate'er the county or dialect.

It is: "Damunblastucumineerubludything".

SAME ADDRESS

So I'm having a pint in the Oak when in comes Geoff Mingay who quickly flogs a draw card in aid of the village soccer team to Gilbert Levitt. Filling in the name and address portion Geoff inquires: "Remind me of your address, Gilbert?" And the reply comes: "You know damn well where I live. I live next door to Ben Blaydon!" And thus it was entered upon the form.

THIRSTING AFTER RIGHTEOUSNESS

There I am, loitering with intent in the Baron of Beef the other Sunday morning when two chaps who play important roles at the University Church of Great St Mary in Cambridge come bowling in after dashing down Trinity Street from the morning service. They launch themselves upon foaming pints with a gleeful ferocity. I know them both well and I enquire of them: "Is this not a perfect example of two good men going to the devil straight from Church?" Not at all, says the very large gentleman. "We are simply thirsting after righteousness."

FRIZ TO THE BARROW

We were a-nattering in the Oak the other day about the bother we all had getting vegetables out of frozen ground during the recent cold snap. My old chum George Ambrose from Swaffham Prior told us how he sweated away hacking at the solid ground to prise up a few parsnips. When, finally, he got them up he couldn't get the frozen soil off them. So he chucked 'em into a metal wheelbarrow hoping they would thaw out a bit." What happened?" asked Percy Blinco. "They friz to the barrow", said George.

THE BARON OF BEEF

Oh, there's danger in the wind, me lads, there's danger in the wind. For the brewers are on the march, me lads, the brewers are on the march...

Yup. I fear it's loin-girding time again for all who love old England and her pubs. You see, the brewers have announced that they plan to spend £1,500 million (say it to yourself slowly: one thousand five hundred million smackeroos) on "refurbishing" Britain's pubs to make then fit for the leisure age. Now if that doesn't send a ripple of horror round the bar nothing will for we all know what it means: false beams, plastic tables, hideous machine games, louder music, desecration of snugs, destruction of dart boards, an end to cribbage and - of course, of course - dearer beer to pay for it all.

Now in the course of my investigative duties I am required to enter upon a large number of licensed premises so that over the years I have become an observant sort of customer and of all the town pubs I know in this part of the world I suppose the most successful one could well be the Baron of Beef in Bridge Street, Cambridge wherein it is possible to find most days a mixture of college dons, undergrads, tourists, itinerant builders, bookies, elegant ladies, wealthy businessmen, the under-worked and the over-paid, the decrepit and the bouncing. To say nothing of the occasional fading hack like yours truly.

In other words it is often packed with as wide a mixture of the drinking public as you are likely to find. And the pub sells a vast amount of beer! Yet, the stentorian landlord Bob Wass whose cry "Last orders please" could awaken the dead would agree that his establishment is slightly jaded, that he has barely touched the decor in the 15 years of his guvnorship and that his bar furniture has remained unaltered in all those years. But therein lies the very reason for the pub's continuing success.

It's a straightforward, unaltered, untidy old boozer and though it sells food that side of the business is an adjunct to flogging beer, not as in so many other pubs, a substitute. He staffs his bar with efficient barmaids (no letters from feminists please; these are real barmaids, not bar persons), refuses to have music other than a good old knees-up around the piano and generally declines to sink with the times.

So, memo to the Brewers Society: hold your next meeting in the Baron of Beef, garrotte all your trendy architects and keep your millions in your pockets. Oh, and yes. With all the money I've saved you, kindly reduce the price of your beer.

THE PUB SIGN

Let me tell you what's happening at the Royal Oak in this parish. The old sign had become somewhat tatty after many years of being buffeted by storm and tempest and parched by summer sun and the momentous decision to repaint it was taken. (We are creatures of stability in this village and even the taking down of a pub sign is a matter for general concern and comment).

Greene King, in their wisdom, have allowed one of the customers, young Dick Bourne, to redesign and repaint the sign and he has come up with the bright and charming idea of painting onto the oak tree the initials of several of the regulars carved into the bark, mine among 'em. Here, then, is an intimation of immortality, for that creaking old sign will certainly outlast most of us and I've no doubt it will still be swinging in the breeze long after we have gone off to that

Great Pub in the Sky where the Landlord never calls time and where he is able with absolute certainty to forecast the winner of the 2.30 at Kempton which is more than Bob Scrutton, landlord of the Oak can do for, despite his encyclopaedic knowledge of the racing world, he could not tip bricks out of a barrow.

DEAD DONKEY

Nattering about the coming year over a jar in the Oak and the old bor Gilbert Levitt sets us all a-thinking when he ups and declares for no particular reason whatsoever: "Three things you won't see in the fen this next twelve month 'cause you've never seen 'em yet - a dead donkey, a humpty-backed gipsy or a satisfied farmer". Reckon he's plumb correct.

THAT PERCY!

Danged if I can get the better of that pesky man Percy Blinco, the Grand Vizier of the Vegetable Patch. I'm rather proud of my leeks and when I blandly lied to him over a pint at the Oak on Sunday that I had dug one up to feed my entire family at lunch he stared me in the face and said without benefit of smile or twinkle: "Nearly left a couple of mine on your back doorstep this morning but I was afraid the weight might have cracked it." I'll have him yet.

KNEES-UP

Participated with gusto t'other evening in a long-lost rite, a pre-gogglebox activity of Edwardian, nay, Victorian overtones. Up at the Oak we decided to rest our pints for a brief while, to lift the lid of the old piano and take down a dusty song-book. And so we indulged ourselves in a discordant but happy, old fashioned sing-song. Marvellous, half-forgotten songs - some boisterous, some jingoistic, some sweetly romantic. Music hall songs, stirring songs from Welsh valleys, eye-misting songs from Scottish hillsides. And, naturally, the poacher's song, which, though from yellow-bellied Lincolnshire, has it own special meaning for several blokes hereabouts. Everyone laughed and had such fun and the beer slaked truly thirsty throats and loosened vocal chords taut from unaccustomed usage. Try it yourselves one of these cold, dark nights. Go on. Turn the box off and have a good old knees-up with the family.

Over a pint in the Oak the other rainy night we fell to bemoaning our financial inability to order decent new suits as of yore, Ranald, the worker-in-wood, told of his Scottish grandfather who would hang his tweeds as others might hang game. He liked to leave a suit unworn for five or six years by which time his tailor would have to "ease" the clothes because of an extended waistline. His ghillie once looked at the old man's decrepit stalking jacket and suggested it was time he wore another adding the sly Scottish warning: "If you hope to get as much wear out of the new as the old you'd better get a move-on at your age".

HARA KIRI

Caught a glimpse of the red shadow of a fox travelling slinkily along the top of the dyke down the fen the other damp evening and later, over a pint, a few of us fell to nattering about Canis vulpes. There was, on the edge of our company, a comparative stranger who asserted that the persecution of the fox was unwarranted for he had it on the strongest authority that Brer Fox was not as voracious as he was painted, that he only killed for food and not for pleasure and that tales of slaughter in hen runs and pheasant coverts were but stories of lummocky countryfolk. Indeed, he declaimed, he knew that chickens actually died of shock when a fox was among them and that was where we old country boys made our error. There was a moment's silence when one who shall remain nameless said quietly: "Clever old birds, they chickens. Not only do they die of shock when they see a fox but they go on afterwards to chop their own heads off and commit hara kiri". At which point the stranger changed the subject.

CHICK'S GOAT

So I'm drowsing the evening away in pleasant conversation with pleasing company and we've settled the world's immediate problems over a couple of pints when Chick Newman mutters casually:

"We've just sent a goat to China". The statement made little impression for we were talking about matters of great import, like whose round was it and was George Weir's ague anything to do with the fact that he had eaten two lobsters over at Brancaster Staithe the day before? You may have gathered that we were sitting in the Oak and I do declare that anyone prepared to lounge in an English pub for half an hour must become disenchanted with the electronic nonsenses of the gogglebox for there was never a scriptwriter born who could match the magnificent, natural inanities of the Britisher at the trough. Slowly, his words sank in and I discarded the lobster problem for a moment and turned to Chick - for, with the inexplicable illogicality of the English nick-name that's what we call this great breeder of goats - and he affirmed that they had indeed exported one of their goats to the great People's Republic of China and for what purpose he was not sure except that they had expressed a profound desire to have it and who was he to stand in the way of the progress of the goat population of that distant land? Having an insatiable curiosity, indeed, to put it not too finely, being nosey to the point of being pushey, I was about to press the matter further when Chick ups and ambles off to a fisherman's meeting in the clubroom upstairs and I learned no more of the exciting odyssey of that ruminant quadruped. But I have fond thoughts of a special, secret department of the intelligence service of that far country devoted to sniffing out the best goat breeders of the fens. Perchance, while Chick and his family were asleep one moonlight night in their small farm between Burwell and Soham some slant-eyed, denim-suited agent had conducted an urgent and furtive midnight survey of his splendid herd. Well, you never know with these wily orientals.

MUM'S VINO

Funny lot, some of the boys I take my beer with down at the Oak. There's dear old Aubrey Ketteridge, for example, whose pride and joy is his garden shed into which is crammed the glorious debris of a lifetime's handywork. He loves working in there - but he will keep locking his keys inside when he leaves. He was at it again last week and twice he was obliged to take the door off to get at "those blasted keys". And then there's young Gilbert Levitt, third best gardener in the village after Percy Blinco and, ahem, one who is reluctant to name himself. Gilbert has rows of peas like hedges, onions like young saplings, taters in tons. Yet in the middle of his flowering broad beans a large strip of land lies strangely fallow. I probed for the reason. Came an embarrassed fit of coughing and then the confession. He had planted his beans, it seems, after enjoying a glass or several of his mother's home-made vino, a substance of gentle and flavoursome taste but ferocious effect. In the gloaming he set his lines, hoed immaculately straight trenches and carefully covered them over again. Unfortunately in six long rows he had quite forgotten to put the beans. Cor, I did laugh.

'WARE SWANS

So there we are, sitting in the Oak all quiet like, watching Phil Coxhead skin a rabbit with the same consummate skill he normally reserves for extracting a pint of mild from me, when, naturally, the talk gets round to swans. Should you be seeking a sense of logic in the foregoing, kindly desist for it's that sort of pub. However, up comes this bloke, a lorry driver, who tells us he has just seen murder done by two swans on a dyke near Ely and I can do no more than record his tale if for no other reason than to rid the townie of the general misconception that the graceful mute swan is a charming and sweet-natured creature. Well, says this chap, an old hare dashes across the road in front of his lorry and disappears over the rim of the steep bank. It runs neither to right nor left and he assumes it must have taken to the water. Being an inquisitive country lad he leaps from his cab and, peering over the bank, finds two swans, a cob and a pen, drowning the hare they have grabbed with their bills. A passing policeman joins him in witnessing the cruel death and it was he who later confirmed the story. So there you are. Next time you cast your bread upon the waters make sure the kiddywinks are standing well back.

PAY UP

Overheard in the Oak t'other day (no names, no packdrill): One ancient to another - "Well, you can't take it with you, bor". Reply from the one with an empty glass - "Then what're you hangin' on to yours for then, bor?"

A LOVING HUSBAND

There is a charming widow over Haddenham way who speaks wistfully and fondly of her departed husband and who tells a tale which I pass on to all male spouses who, like him, might occasionally incur the wrath of the distaff side by lingering longingly over that last luscious pint instead of beating an earlier retreat from the village hostelry. The lady in question had issued a series of warnings about her husband's behaviour, and finally determined to follow up her verbal assaults with the real thing and, as midnight approached, she positioned herself behind the front door as, slowly weaving, he neared home. When he stepped over the threshold he found his wife standing with rolling pin upraised but before the admonishing blow could be delivered he took her gently by the arm and said lovingly: "Now then, my dear, it's far too late for you to be a-baking. Come you on to bed."

"And", says his widow, "he said it so nice and kindly I never did have the heart to belt him one."

Food and Drink

MARVELLOUS MORELS

I fear that with one careless swish of the quill I am about to write out of my life one of the world's greatest delicacies and one after which I lust each succeeding spring.

Naturally I refer to the luscious morel which is, and I refuse to be gainsayed, quite the most delicious of all the mushrooms. It is rare and getting rarer and it's due to make its annual appearance any time now.

I count myself one of God's luckier creatures because occasionally I am delivered of a bag of 'em by my old friend from Babraham, John Robinson - a man who, so long as he keeps bringing them to me, is at once kindly, erudite, handsome, charming, sophisticated, loyal, witty and fearless. He has a secret source of the marvellous morel and some readers will recall that last year he asked me to pass a quantity of them on to my long-time companion in gastronomic debauchery, Douglas Gibson. I stole them and ate them and I hereby give public notice that given half a chance I shall do so again.

Perhaps, I prayed, John might remember me again this year and then once more my cup of gladness, my bowl of delight, would certainly run over. But here comes the line which will ruin my chances. For I hear that the morel is now in such short supply and in such long demand that specialist food shops are prepared to pay £20 a pound for them.

Yes, twenty quid for a pound of mushrooms. Twenty jimmy-o-goblins, 400 shillings, 200 florins, a whole lak of rupees. Now when this intelligence is brought before the good Mr Robinson I suppose he will seek to convert his morels into filthy lucre rather than provide his mates with a little creature comfort.

But if he does I now issue another public notice: I shall withdraw my previous description of him and reveal to you the real truth...

PUDDEN CLUB

I would not wish the secret I am about to share with you to be bruited abroad, promulgated widely, bandied about or in any way circulated among the general public for if the crime I have just committed this cold and frosty morning were to become general knowledge then 'twould be the tumbril for me and no doubting it, me hearties.

For (and whisper it low) I have just partaken of a proper breakfast; an English breakfast; what Izaak Walton called in his "Compleat Angler" a "good, honest, wholesome, hungry breakfast".

And that is a crime, you say? Well, 'fraid so. For in these days of bran and yoghurt, muesli and dried fruit, polyunsaturates and skimmed milk, these butterless, meatless days, the state guillotine is raised high and ready for the peasant who dares to tread the culinary path of his forebears.

And because of the constant exhortations to throw over the English brekker and eat instead like a skinny squirrel we in this household have, since the excesses of Christmas, been sliding the odd spoonful of mixed nuts and oats down past the larynx at breakfast time and a roughage time has been had by one and all.

However, there are still pockets of resistance around and one leader of a particularly virulent group of fighters in the Freedom for Flab campaign is my old mate (young mate, actually), Paul Harris, a denizen of the Baron of Beef hostelry in Cambridge.

Upon his occasional forays into the wilds of the midlands and the north Paul wisely buys up large portions of black pudding and, being a good lad, often bungs me a ring or two of the northern glory.

He presented me with a lump this weekend and I popped it into the fridge so that it would not tempt me away from the muesli.

Nevertheless, as I walked through the cold gale this morning and tramped off down the fen I realised again that the only way to get rid of temptation is to yield to it and upon return to the warm kitchen I gave the muesli its marching orders and turned for succour to Newmarket sausages, the black pudding, golden eggs laid by contented hens and toast soggy with butter. Tally ho, yoicks and let 'em all come. I'm ready to take on the Red hordes with one arm tied behind me back.

Of course, I'm not advocating that we all nosh like that every day of our lives and I'm not trying to bring on a general coronary. But, cor, it ain't half nice now and again.

There is another side to this black pudding caper which should not be overlooked. You see, the aforementioned Paul Harris and I, though friends for years, are at different ends of the political line and he thinks that I am on the far right of Genghis Khan while I think he makes Stalin look like Michael Heseltine. But black pudding unites us, frees us from the fetters of extremism, removes the scales from our biased eyes and allows us to live in the harmony of the brotherhood of the Pudden Club.

JAM TODAY - AND TOMORROW

That great-uncle of mine - he married, late in life, a lady of ample proportions and half his age and died soon afterwards with a wide smile on his face - always maintained that life's simpler pleasures were the most flavoursome and I have never found reason to gainsay him.

Thus you will understand that last week for me was a good 'un if for no other reason than that I found ten jars of long-lost strawberry jam.

You see, the rambling old house which we Jeacocks infest has more cupboards to the square yard than ever poor Mrs Hubbard could have dreamt about and each one is stuffed with the detritus left behind in the wake of my long marrige to Squirrel Nutkin. Herself loves shoving things into the cupboards because "they'll come in handy for the children one day" though what they will do with about three thousand assorted and worn out shirts, pants and socks is beyond me.

And though we can never find anything we're looking for, there nevertheless is a feeling of adventure when involved in any search of our cupboards, for who knows what will come to the surface.

Well, hidden behind some of my wine-making equipment, I'm happy to report, were those jars of lovely jam which herself made from last year's crop. The jam is in two-pound jars and that's a lot of jam. But why, I inquired, had she hidden it? She hadn't hidden it, she said, she'd simply forgotten about it. How could she forget twenty pounds of jam, I wondered aloud? She replied, with that sense of logic for which she is justly famous in six counties: "As a matter of fact I forgot about the damson jam in the dining room cupboard as well." At which point I buttered me toast and plastered it with the new found treasure trove and marvelled silently.

Later there was a goosegog pie in the oven and we picked the first of our raspberries - and what raspberries! Our canes are in their third year and they have gone potty. I can eat 'em three times a day without getting fed up but there'll be too many even for me. So, I suggested to herself that she might like to make a few pounds of jam. So we can put it in another cupboard. And forget about it.

BEAST OF BRIDGE STREET

My fondness for food leads to many kindnesses from some friends and a large amount of double dealing from others. Last week: Toby Joseph was on a business trip in Derbyshire and went thirty miles out of his way to buy me a pork pie in Bakewell. He left it with Bob Wass, landlord of the Baron of Beef in Cambridge for me to collect. Wass, The Beast of Bridge Street, scoffed it before I got there. Don Misson, ex-landlord of The Bakers Arms at Fulbourn makes a magnificent brawn. He left a tray of it for me in the Royal Oak here in the village. Bob Thomson, Ranald Scott and Stevie Marsh demolished it in the bar before I could get it home.

EGGS FOR BREAKFAST - IN SHERRY

And mention of breakfasts brings me to a chap by the name of Geoff Blackwell. I bumped into him on Saturday night in a Derbyshire pub which I haunted in my distant youth and at first, in the dim light and due to the fact that I hadn't seen him for at least forty years, I did not recognise him. He heard my name mentioned, however, realised who I was and reminded me that as a boy I used to run his sheep from the hills down into Bakewell market. (It was our job as lads to run on ahead of the flocks of sheep to make sure the field and garden gates were closed to keep those cunning animals on the road - four mile run to market, four mile walk home. Pay? A tanner). Geoff is now well beyond his three score years and ten and I congratulated him upon his obvious good health.

"It is all due", he said slowly as they do in Derbyshire, "to what I 'ave fer me breakfast". I assumed I was about to hear the sort of tale I have been telling in my previous paragraphs. But no.

"Always, ave two eggs"' he went on. "Boiled?", I asked. "Raw", he replied. There was a pause. "In 'alf a pint of sherry. Stirred up. Every day." There was a further pause while he drained his whisky and washed it down with a huge suck of beer. "Got to be right sort of sherry", he said. "None of that foreign muck".

FLAMBEED KIPPERS

Back to kippers. I asked recently if there were more exciting ways of cooking 'em than the dull ones we all know and it comes to pass that I bump into that enterprising, innovatory and constantly vocal young(ish) Irish chef who delights customers at the Cambridge Lodge Hotel with his culinary novelties, Mr Pat Collins himself, and the man says to me in between slurps of the Guinness that didn't his father, God bless him, once upon a time chuck the kippers on to the grill and then flambe them with a quick dose of the whiskey (note the spelling) before tucking into them with freshly made horseradish sauce as the accompaniment and wasn't that the most darlin' manner to begin the devilishly difficult day but make sure 'tis Irish whiskey and mine's another pint of the black stuff Michael me boy, says he to meself.

SPARROWGRASS SOLDIERS

When I returned from my walk dampened and dispirited, herself first accused me of being as grave as a mustard pot and then thawed my misery by offering me an angel's breakfast. Simple but superb. A couple of fresh eggs, lightly boiled, with hot spears of newly-cut asparagus for use as dunking soldiers. The Times gave it as a recipe this week but we've been glorying in this joyful repast for years.

TONIC - OR LOBSTER?

In a week when it is cold enough to freeze cricket off Fenner's and the Cambridge Economic Policy Group forecast 4.3 million unemployed by 1985 it seems only reasonable to seek refuge in the pursuit of hedonism which, as you know, is the belief that pleasure is the chief good.

Which takes me immediately to lobsters and my spanking new

economic theory which will give many of you a chance to explore new gourmet delights and leave you with cash over for other joys. The new theory is based on the principle of subsituting a greater pleasure for a lesser one, and the idea came to me in a sudden blinding flash of inspiration when I was talking to a depressed Cambridge businessman about the cost of lobsters.

He had just left Cambridge market where, on one of the two excellent fish stalls, he had spied the legend "Lobster - £3.60 a pound" and as he ordered his third gin and tonic he deplored his financial inability to obtain his favourite crustacean. I stopped his doleful monologue in mid-sentence and queried the number of gins he drank daily. Three before lunch and three before dinner on weekdays and a few more at the weekends, he confessed.

And each with a bottle of tonic costing on average 20p a bottle, I said, adding (for by now lightning had struck) that he was spending more than £9.00 a week on tonic water.

Anxious not to deny his daily injection I urged upon him the wisdom of switching to pink gins with their rich overtones of naval wardrooms and days of imperial grandeur. "Nine oncers a week", said I. "Thirty-six jimmy-o-goblins a month". "Some four hundred and seventy smackers per annum". His eyes grew round and I ordered him a pink gin and he began to speak softly of weekly mounds of lobster a la Broche, a la Newburg, au Gratin, a la Russe....

PORT AND PEACE

Cancel the nuclear shelter. Sing hey-nonny-no and start saving again for I have proof that the future is safe. Well, the next twenty years at least. What makes me so certain? I will share the secret with you before passing it on to Whitehall. A friendly Fellow of Trinity tells me his college has just laid down a new pipe of vintage port (a pipe is about 115 Imperial gallons, if my friends of the Left will excuse the description) which will sleep in the cellars until 2001 by which time it will have matured to perfection. Now these Trinity Fellows are a canny lot with friends in high places and any chance of war, revolution or plague coming between them and the pulling of port corks in the next century would have had them buying an earlier vintage. So relax.

AN ODE TO ASPARAGUS

Should all nine daughters of Zeus and Mnemosyne flock to my side determined to inspire me to pen the greatest ode of all history I fear I should disappoint them something rotten, as the Greeks say, by choosing as my subject - asparagus. I would offer to the world an address to that simple vegetable in a style so exalted that the taste-buds of continents would re-awaken, the sated would be driven to fresh hunger and governments would fall should they not supply asparagus on the National Health, free. I would urge, in lilting phrase, the delights of abnegation during ten months of the year for the home-grown asparagus season is but a short one. The lustful gaze should be averted from the pale imports from our former colonies for, good though some may find the produce of California, I would declare with resounding clarity that nothing compares with that old sparrow-grass freshly cut from a fenland garden. Now before I get too carried away let me admit, be it not already discernable, that I'm half partial to asparagus and I am driven to verbal excess because I have just eaten the first decent bait of it from our own garden. We have a couple of modest beds - my first priority when I took over the house was to bung in some lovely crowns I bought over at Isleham where they know a thing or three about asparagus - and they yield about sixty pounds a season. I have been known to give some of it away although I always shed a bitter tear when I part with it but with the starving hordes which infest this establishment we tend to have at it rather hard. It comes to table hot, with plain melted butter, Hollandaise, Maltese and Mousseline sauces or, perhaps a Bearnaise sauce minus the herbs; cold , with oil and vinegar, mayonnaise - try it Chantilly style with beaten cream added - and aioli. We eat it in tarts, in scrambled eggs (with a touch of french mustard beaten in), we scoff it au gratin with the tips lightly covered with Mornay sauce and Parmesan cheese sprinkled and glazing under nubs of melting butter. And to wash it down? Nowt wrong with cider, of course. But nothing to beat something from the Loire, a Pouilly Fume or a Sancerre, unless it be a Tokay d'Alsace, full-bodied but not sweet yet strong enough to fight a gentle battle with any of the sauces.

Escoffier gives a recipe for asparagus ice-cream. I have not tried it for it sounds a bit too frogified for me and in no way would it appear in my ode of praise to the vernal shoots of this emperor of vegetables.

Having said all that I must admit that the two cartons of mushy peas and dollops of mint sauce plopped on top which I hogged at Reach Fair on Monday didn't half go down a treat. I was tempted to try a third lot but caution defeated gluttony.

BLACK PUDDING AND BRAWN

When those pesky candidates come knocking at your door next week or two grab 'em by the rosettes and demand of them what they propose to do about the rotten black puddings we voters are forced to endure in Cambridgeshire. Ignore their protestations that there are more important matters at the heart of this election and force from them a firm and unequivocable answer for the state of the black pudding scene is little less than a regional disgrace. I say this in the knowledge that there is nothing more terrifying than the sight of pork butchers in full fury but although I may face the prospect of being garrotted by one with sausage skin I must declare in the interests of gastronomic truth that as producers of that superb delicacy they are the flops. The reasons why I am in such a flavver is that I have just scoffed a couple of horse-shoe-shaped puddings made by a butcher in the town of Buxton, high in the Derbyshire Peak District and brought to me by my friend and fellow gourmand, Maurice Squires who nips out from his carpet shop in Cherryhinton Road, Cambridge, occasionally for a taste of the good things in life. When I heard he was off north on business I implored him to relieve me of my deepest frustrations by bringing back to me the black puddings of luscious memory. He did more. He cleared the dazed butcher of his entire stock of the aforementiond delicacy and handed them around to his other chums in beleaguered Cantab. Thus much pleasure was brought south. Alas, it was followed by piteous complaints as to why our local butchers cannot tempt us with such heavenly pudding. Or are we being unfair?

And to pile calumny upon insult let me add that it's difficult to find a half tidy bowl of brawn in these parts. Which is odd, really, since Cambridgeshire was noted for its brawn - they call it pork cheese hereabouts but more of that later - especially in between the great wars. There are old folk about who still remember their parents talking of the brawn made before the turn of the century at the Rose Inn at Stapleford which was trundled into Cambridge and sold at the Old Bell on Peas Hill. Time, of course, adds flavour to truth, but for the legend to have lasted so long it must have been quite a dish.

I reckon pork cheese and brawn are completely different dishes and not just differing regional names for the same nosh. The lowly Cambridgeshire pork cheese is made from pig's head alone while real brawn, says I, is ennobled by the addition of pigs trotters and some shin beef. Danged if I don't get the missus to knock some up for me. Brawn, that is, not pork cheese.

COW 'EEL

As for those wretched black puddings, I'm beginning to wish I hadn't mentioned 'em last week. I've been inundated with pleas from expatriate northerners to put them on the track of a decent southern pudding but, alas, I have had to send them on their way weeping. One Mr Burnett of Cambridge, who sounded solidly Yorkshire when he phoned me, told me he had drooled when he read of my Derbyshire puds and then went on to impart the almost totally useless information that whilst on holiday with relatives in Gibraltar he had come across some of the best black puddings of a lifetime. On second thoughts, my lads, 'ow about a coach trip to Gib for a day on the puddings and ale?

And as for brawn I swear I never will mention it again anywhere. Everybody, it seems, has his or her own idea how it should be made. I suggested that real brawn needed the addition of pigs trotters to achieve total nobility. But that led to cries of 'traitor' and other words which I chose not to decipher when I met Lancastrian Alan Burns in the Oak. "Nay lad", he said, or words to that effect, "nay lad. Tha' means cow 'eel. You can't 'ave brawn wi'out cow 'eel".

MULBERRIES, HONEY AND CREAM

And so to mulberries. There is an old and magnificently-burdened mulberry overhanging an ancient clunch wall in the garden of a friendly neighbour just up the village street and on Sunday we were invited to pick from the crop to our hearts' - and stomachs' - content. We haven't chomped on the rich juiciness of the mulberry since that fine tree in the garden of the County Farmers' Club in Cambridge literally went with the wind some years ago. A storm blew it over and took away a small slice of heaven. But on Sunday our pudding bowls were heaped high. And to go with the huge fruits just fresh cream and new honey from our own busy hive to ward off the tartness.

TIPSY PIGEONS

To hang or not to hang, that is the question which has to be faced as we slither towards winter. It is a matter upon which the nation must decide ere long and without more ado for time is of the essence, my bonnies, and for too long the subject has been shirked with a frightening irresponsibility. I refer, naturally, to game; pheasant, partridge, grouse, hare, all those robust ingredients of great meals with which we fend off the offending vapours of chill autumn days. Now I am a hanging man myself, for in my view there is no gameiness in game unless the beast has been brought to that perfection of 'highness' which translates the ordinary into the fabulous. Thus is it a ridiculous nonsense for the more showy of our restaurateurs to offer their customers grouse on the Glorious Twelfth - just as well flog them a platter of mushy cotton wool. Nope. Won't have it otherwise - there is no taste in pheasants roasted the day after having met their fate, in partridges basted before they've been around for a week or in hare which is eaten as quick as if it were a mere conie.

Having thus made my position clear I hasten to add that in a lifetime of shooting and eating my quarry I have never yet met anyone who has come up with clearly defined theories about the length of time the prey should be hung and since there are so many variants involved - temperature, humidity, personal taste - I don't suppose I ever will. But to young housewives about to launch themselves into that most important side of married life, the grubstakes, I would say this: when there's frost in the air let those pheasants hang for four or five days in a well-ventilated place before stuffing them with halved grapes and roasting them. There'll be no frostiness about the house and you'll have started the old man off on the trail of pleasure which comes round annually at the commencement of the game season.

One thing is for sure this year - you won't be feeding the old codger on grouse for they are so scarce I hear some of the posher shops are chopping them out at £40 a brace. So, for the big treat try this recipe which comes to me via Tim Brown of Girton, a bloke of sober and abstemious habits in all things other than the eating of pigeons in which matter he is something of a glutton. He calls the dish "Tipsy Pigeons" and it serves two. Take - 8 black olives, 4tbl spns dry sherry, 2 pigeons, 2tbl spns oil, 1 onion sliced, 4oz bacon rinded and chopped, 4 slices garlic sausage, 3 level tbl spns flour, half pint chicken stock, 2tbl spns brandy. Marinade olives in sherry for 2 hours. Fry pigeons in oil until golden brown - about 5 minutes. Drain and put in casserole. Fry onion, bacon and garlic sausage in remaining fat until also golden brown - about 5 minutes. Remove from pan with slotted spoon and add to casserole with sherry and olives. Stir flour into fat remaining in pan and cook for 2-3 minutes. Gradually stir in the stock, bring to boil and stir until it thickens. Add brandy, salt and pepper and pour over pigeons. Cover and cook in oven at 170 deg C (325 deg F), Mark 3 for one and a half hours until tender. Warning: it's exceedingly rich. And P.S.: don't bother to hang the pigeons, they don't need it.

DRINKING LAMBSWOOL

Let us then abandon our worries about the sliding pound, the nauseous Scargill, the unstoppable West Indians and concentrate upon an unsolved problem of vital importance which has clues pointing to the giant Emperor Maximinus, the Catherine wheel, old Sam Pepys and a strange, ancient drink invented by the Celts.

The problem - it's worrying me to death - is simply this: which Cambridge college still drinks "lambswool" at Lammastide which is fast approaching?

The question arises because Miss Leila Brown, of St Matthew's Street, Cambridge, has written to me asking if I know the answer for she, too, is desperate to set her mind at ease.

She read in "Shakespeare's Flowers" by Jessica Kerr a reference to "lambswool" which has nothing to do with the animal or its coat but is in fact a brew consisting of ale, nutmeg, sugar and toasted crab apples which the authoress declares is still served by a Cambridge college on the feast day of Lammastide - August 1.

Well, the good Miss Brown has tried several of the older colleges but they deny any knowledge of the custom and knowing that I have a mind stuffed with utterly useless information she turned to me.

Alas, I don't know either. But I do know that on St Catherine's day in November there are still some children of Worcestershire who go 'Catherning' - demanding gifts of apples and money and that once upon a time spinsters of that lovely county would roast apples before the fire until the pulp fell into a bowl called a Cathern bowl. And guess what was in the bowl? Why, ale and spices and sugar. And guess what the mixture was called? Why "lambswool", of course.

So what's the connection with Gaius Julius Verus Maximinus, the barbarous soldier who became Emperor of Rome in AD 235? Well, without him we wouldn't have had St Catherine for it was he who had her beheaded after she had defended the Christian faith in a discussion with heathen philosophers. (At the time she was bound to a wheel upon which her bonds miraculously parted, hence the catherine wheel!)

And where's the connection with Samuel Pepys? Well, in the dim recesses of my strange mind I faintly recall the diarist mentioning the drink which was, in fact, an invention of the Celts to whom it was known as "Lamasaghet".

But none of this leads us to the Cambridge college wherein it is still drunk. And it is important for us to know not only because Miss Brown and I are getting into a tizzy about it but because mine host at that excellent establishment, the Fox Inn at Longstowe, has threatened to make the brew if a proper recipe can be produced. So if there's anyone in the Local Brain Unit who can help let him not be backward at coming forward with the answer.

AND MAKING IT

And so back to lambs-wool and what an erudite lot you are. Three weeks ago I asked a few questions about "lambswool" which is an old English drink and though none of you could tell me which Cambridge college still drinks it at Lammastide (and I still can't find out so I suspect the custom has withered) lots of you came up with fascinating historical background on the tipple. Pepys referred to it in

Vol VIII of his Diary; it turns up in Shakespeare - in "Love's Labour's Lost" and "Midsummer Night's Dream"; Eric Linklater said it should be drunk in the "silence of appreciation and the quietness of content"; it was drunk in south Staffordshire in a ceremony called "Clemeny" and the Irish drank it at the feast of apple gathering called in Irish "La mas cibhal", pronounced "Lammas ool" and corrupted into "lamb-swool".

There's much much more so it must have been a popular drink and here is Robert Carrier's recipe for it: for 10-12 drinks take - two and a half pints of old ale, 60 cloves, 10 cooking apples cored, 2 teaspoons ground ginger, 2 teaspoons freshly grated nutmeg, brown sugar to taste.

Stick 6 cloves in each apple, bake in moderate oven until cooked thoroughly, sieve into large pan adding beer, spices and sweetener. Heat carefully. Cheers.

SWEET SLOE GIN

"There are slivers of frost on the ploughed black fen
And a sniff of snow from some distant glen.
So beware, my friends, lest your blood run thin.
And turn your thoughts to sweet sloe gin".

Pray, brave literati and know-alls, whence these charming lines? Which writer of subtle elegance, which spurned poet or raffish boulevardier, which sadly undiscovered genius and caster of pearls ushered them into the breathless and waiting world?

Right first time. 'Twere me. My inspiration came this fine and frosty Monday morn when I staggered into the kitchen after a crisp walk and a touch of axework. There, warming itself into maturity, was my damn great jar of sloe gin, purple as a duke's face, tempting as a treacle tart, inviting as a four-poster.

Yet, alas and alack, as yet untouchable for it wants another month at least of patience on my part and steeping on its own before I can have at it. Like Wilde, I can resist everything except temptation and I have this mounting feeling of inevitability creeping upon me. A few more sharp frosts and high resolution will wilt and some of that glorious nectar will perish in its youth, slightly callow mayhap but warming nevertheless.

I seem to recall that when they excavated a Neolithic village at Glastonbury some years ago they found whole barrowloads of sloe stones which indicated that our grandads were more than somewhat keen on these tart and, to us, uneatable wild plums. Did they have a recipe for cooking 'em which we have never discovered? Or was there some smart Dutchman wandering around Somerset in those days flogging 'em mashed juniper berries?

MINNOWS AND PAIGLES

Our paigles - others know them as cowslips - are slowly spreading in the orchard and one spring soon there will be a mass of wobbling, golden heads. I haven't tasted cowslip wine for many a year and because the plant is now so rare I don't suppose I ever will for it seems insensitive to say the least to pick them for a private pleasure.

There is a little-known recipe hiding away in Izaak Walton's "The Compleat Angler" in which the cowslip blossom plays an important part. He discusses minnows and says:

"He (the minnow) is a sharp biter at a small worm, and in hot weather makes excellent sport for young anglers, or boys, or women that love that recreation, and in the spring they make of them excellent minnow-tansies; for being washed well in salt, and their heads and tails cut off, and their guts taken out, and not washed after, they prove excellent for that use; that is being fried with yolk of eggs, the flowers of cowslips and of primroses, and a little tansy; thus used they do make a dainty dish of meat."

Sounds quite charming but I think I'll stick to a platter of salmon mousse with lobster sauce if it's all the same by you, Izaak, me old son.

I'm not quite as enthusiastic about the survival of borage in the garden as I am about the paigles in the orchard even though in medieval times borage was known as an efficient aphrodisiac. Madame introduced it into her herb garden (why, I wonder?) and the damned stuff has now spread into my best asparagus bed and although I have addressed it in severe yet simple terms it ignores me and continues its onward march.

Nevertheless, this herbal equivalent of powdered rhinoceros

horn, is a pretty enough plant and its blue, starry flowers make a delicious addition to summer drinks, particularly Pimms, while its young leaves can be placed in hot water and used as an inhalant to cure the resulting hangover.

THREE TIMES A DAY!

A reader asks me why I spend so much of my time writing about the joys of food. There is a simple answer and I rumbled it when I was but a slender sapling myself. Eating is the only major human pleasure which can be indulged in satisfactorily three times a day from birth to senility. Satisfactorily, I said.

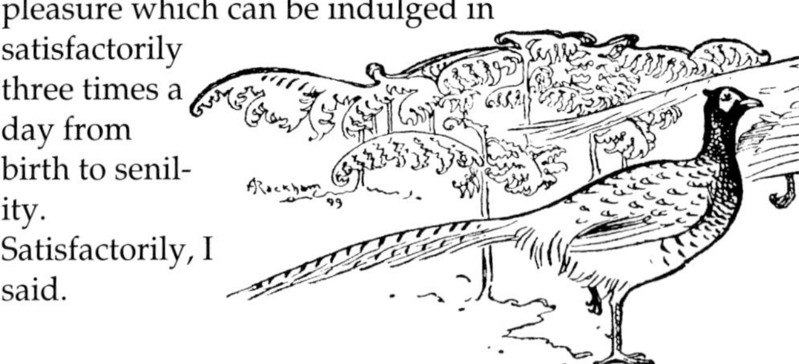

Herself and Others

WISE OLD PRAWN

"It would appear", said the lady in the blue hat in Ely Cathedral on Saturday night, "that you are a simple soul". The lady in question was addressing herself to me at the time and, despite an urgent search of the old brain box I found that I could not bring myself truthfully to rebut the accusation.

I awaited the next sally with some apprehension. Thankfully, she was a kindly person, despite her apparent prescience, and she continued: "What I really mean is that you seem to find great pleasure in the simpler things in life which must make you a very contented man."

Well, I couldn't deny that either and I felt slightly mollified despite the fact that her first statement had for ever shattered my self-illusion of being a sophisticate, a sage, and yea verily, even an oracle.

We were talking during the interval of the splendid Celebrity Concert in the Cathedral to which my wife and I had repaired to listen to the Central Band of the Royal Air Force and the Royal Choral Society and later, as herself and I were working our way through a post-concert Chinese nosh of immense subtlety at the Peking Duck, I mentioned the lady's remarks.

She paused, picked up a large prawn with her chopsticks and said, in a tone which would have done credit to Confucius: "Comfort yourself, my dear. It is good to converse with a mind that is grandly simple." She then ate the prawn (the last one - I had been saving it for myself) before adding: "It is written that the wise, through excess of wisdom, is made a fool; a fate, my dear, quite unlikely to befall you".

HAPPINESS IN A BOTTLE

Let us now turn to the annual nightmare. It's the birthday of herself this week and what, I ask myself every year at this time, does one give to a woman who claims to have nothing? (At this stage of the paragraph I find it necessary to take extreme care with my words for when, a year or two back, I wrote in this column that because it was her birthday, I was allowing my wife a day off from the hewing of wood and the drawing of water, one lady in Huntingdon actually took me at my word and wrote me a letter of such startling malevolence, in which I was called every sort of male chauvinist pig, that I am still half afraid of visiting that fair town lest she recognise me for she would undoubtedly behead me.)

Nope. The giving of gifts to one with whom one has shared half of one's existence becomes increasingly difficult. "Rich gifts wax poor when givers prove unkind", somebody said in Hamlet, and though I've no intention of being unkind (well, not on her birthday, lady from Huntingdon), neither have I the means for rich gifts.

It is, however, my view that the greatest of all gifts is that of happiness. And since in marriage happiness stems from seeing one's spouse happy I believe I have found a solution.

Herself knows of my great fondness for fine claret. Therefore, upon her birthday I will open the very last bottle of my 1961 Gruaud Larose. I will decant it. I will sniff it, sip it, quaff it. I will encourage her to watch joy spread over my visage as I finish the decanter all by myself. Thus will she witness my great pleasure and in so doing she will be happy for me. Thus will I have awarded her the gift of happiness on her birthday. Yes. That's what I'll do.

Actually, lady from Huntingdon, before you take pen to paper I should tell you I've really bought her something quite jolly. So there.

PLAIN BATTY

That old harvest moon has been shining his head off these past few nights casting a delicious glow over the land and before we wax too lyrical let me admit that I never see the harvest moon without thinking of the marital bed.

You see, 'tis an old Fenland belief that September is one of the luckiest months in which to be wedded because, they say, if the harvest moon should shine upon the bed of a newly-married couple then they will both be blessed with a long and happy life.

However, there is nothing in Fenland lore so far as I can discover which deals with the results of the harvest moon shining down upon the bed of a couple who have been married for a quarter of a century or so (I never can remember when we went to the altar) though from an experience of ours the other night I suspect that the moon loses its power for benevolence as the years pass.

It was in this wise: after a stroll in the light of the moon followed by a soothing glass of the '83 elderberry wine - the former golden as a wedding ring, the latter purple as a bishop's nose - I slipped into bed ready as ever for instant oblivion.

The windows were open and into our cavernous old bedroom the light of the moon shone and that was the last, peaceful, blissful thing I remember until The Incident.

Herself, you understand, likes to read before nodding off and currently she is ploughing through Daphne Du Maurier's "Vanishing Cornwall". On The Night, herself had, apparently, just reached that part of the book in which there are tales of drowned sailors wrecked on the Cornish coast and of their ghosts wandering ashore when my joyful kip was ended by an ungodly shriek.

"A bat", she screamed. "A huge bat".

Now in the hazy panic of awakening from that first and deepest of sleeps I misunderstood the lady and immediately assumed that she was returning, for some obscure reason at that time of night, to that unshaken belief to which she has clung throughout our married life which is that I am batty.

And for a few moments I lay doggo trying to remember what clanger, what blunder, what heresy I might have committed during the day which could possibly have given birth to this explosive howl.

Then I saw the shadow of the poor bat as it swept and swirled its terrified way around the bedroom, shadows which I admit were much magnified by the bedside lights.

"Calm yourself, my dear", I said - or words to that effect - "for bats are the friendliest of creatures and there is no need to be alarmed."

"There is", came her muffled cry from the depths of the bed, "when your mind is full of ghostly Cornish sailors".

Oddly enough, I'm not much of a batman myself and what is more I happen to be the President of the British League of Cowards so I summoned son Simon and daughter Naomi to our bedroom to see this natural phenomenon for themselves whilst I went below decks to find a suitable box with which to capture and remove the creature, hoping of course that one or t'other of the kids would have done the task before my return.

And, lo, Simon the Brave had taken the bat in his hand and had released it into the moonlit night for it to continue with its insectivorous activities.

Thus was peace restored to the house though it must be said that herself read no more that night and we slept for the first time in years with the windows firmly closed.

SIMSIM

Pause here for a self-satisfied smirk. You see, my son Simon was afflicted when a tiny lad by having his Ma and his three sisters call him by the baby name of "Simsim". As he grew older the name haunted the poor lad and we had almost forgotten it until last week when I spotted a nag in the list of runners and riders called, would you believe it "Simsim". Now, unless my memory fails me, and it doesn't, I cannot recall my son and heir actually pushing any spondulicks in my direction in the whole of his life but here was a one-off chance of exploiting the poor fellow's youthful embarrassment. So I backed the beast. And, lo and behold, it won. My son's immediate and urgent appeal for me to bung him a fiver out of the winnings fell upon exceedingly deaf ears.

STIR-UP-SUNDAY

Much consternation in our household when the married woman with whom I have been living these past 25 years discovered that we had let "Stir Up Sunday" slip by this year without making the Christmas puds. The missus is very much a traditionalist when it comes to Christmas and the entire family - excluding, alack, mad Sam the World's Worst Gundog, Sebastian Herbert the crazed cat, Peter the screeching budgie and Ferdinand and Ferocious Fred the fanatical Fenland ferrets - is obliged annually to stir the puddings whilst making a wish. No matter if the kiddleywinks are away on their endless journeying they are still required to make contact with the Head Girl who stirs madly away by proxy whilst the wishes are whispered. Last year number two daughter Rachel, away at her studies in York, received a message to phone home urgently. She dashed to the phone fearing a family disaster only to find mother stirring the puddings on her behalf and waiting for the wish to be made. Anyway, the whole ceremony is a waste of time for me because my wish never comes true. I'm still waiting to get one of those little silver things in my portion of pudding.

COSTLY DONKEY

Now, I have not only an eye for a pretty lady but also for a classy horse which is why last week I took my daft number one daughter to Tattersall's sale ring at Newmarket to teach her a few things about the top end of the equine market. Twas the end of the sales and nags were being flogged for a few hundred guineas when into the ring was led, or rather, dragged, what on first appearances was a donkey, a ragamuffin of a beast. Ho-ho, I say to Sarah, this disgusting tin of dog-meat will never even reach the £500 mark. Why do people inflict this sort of nonsense upon the buyers? The bidding started at £7,000 and when it reached £17,000 I walked away with Sarah's mocking giggles ringing in my ears. Idiocy would seem to be my speciality.

THE ICE MAIDEN

Herself is a splendid skater but she has not been terribly keen on practising the art in my presence for quite a few years. You see, when we came out into the fens I had to learn how to skate and she very kindly offered to help me stand up on the thin blades. Or that was the general intention. In fact, no sooner had I wobbled onto the ice being held firmly by her than, kerrunch, I fell upon the dear lady, pinning her to the ice.

I fell upon her, you understand, not with any weird intent; more with a succession of fearsome oaths and since in matters of physical size we are at different ends of the scales you will gather there was little pleasure in the operation for her. The collision was the equivalent of a tiny sailing dinghy being run over by the QE2 or the crushing of a butterfly by a passing mammoth and the result, alas, was that the old gel was obliged to spend a week in bed with damaged vertebrae. Thus these days whenever we take to the ice she hurtles off in order to distance herself from me and I am abandoned and left to flounder about and fall down on my own like some vast, drunken, geriatric walrus.

A LONG DROP

Never eaten guinea fowl eggs until this week when Peter Singleton presented me with a dozen. They are rich and delicious, yolks the colour of the setting sun. Very hard shells, they have. Herself asked me why so at breakfast. Because, I said, in their native Guinea the ground is further away from the bird's laying mechanism than here in England. She gave me a withering look of disbelief.

TO DRINK OR TO DIG?

The kiddleywinks were asking what I would like for my forthcoming birthday and I suggested some wine since the wooden case comes in handy for kindling. Had I something in mind, they wondered? A modicum of claret, quoth I, pointing to Adnams splendid new wine list on page 20 of which they are offering a 1949 Chateau La Mission Haut-Brion at a modest £1311.00 a dozen, a trifling £109.00 a bottle. The silence was broken by Naomi asking if perhaps a nice, new trowel might not be somewhat more practical.

POTTY

On one of those really hot days last week herself and I sat out in the garden for the first time this year. I fell asleep in the strange sunshine and I awoke to the laughter of our neighbour Mrs Mollie Stuart. She had strolled into the garden to find me asleep and my missus sitting there sandpapering our downstairs lavatory seat. It's a rather grand mahogany job which some twerp painted. Now she wants to return it to its former glory and she is given to attacking it at the most peculiar moments. And she wonders why people think she is potty.

TOOTHPASTE HOUSE

D'you recall Miss Squirrel Nutkin, she of the gathering and hoarding variety? Yes? Well I married her.

Or so it could be argued by even the most casual observer. For my missus is utterly incapable of parting with the most useless, unserviceable, superfluous, dispensable, worthless piece of furniture, utensil or chattel which we have collected over the long years of our cohabitation.

Thus you may imagine my horror upon being ordered by her to travel north and bring home a huge vanload of family furniture which is lately come into her possession. It now stands in the house blocking hall, passage, drawing room, dining room - you name it, she's filled it.

This family of ours is like a tube of toothpaste being squeezed by the powerful pressure of unwanted furniture. One more blasted chaise longue and we will all be shot out of the back door.

PASSION

We've just had a series of family photographs taken and one of them shows me standing in my pompous father pose holding the hand of the mother of our children. Number three daughter Naomi glanced at the picture and, astonsihed by the apparent display of friendship 'twixt the missus and me, blurted out: "I'll bet that's the most passionate thing you two have done in the last 20 years".

THUNDER OF TINY FEET

In one of the glossy Sunday magazines last weekend the Duchess of Devonshire was quoted as saying how convenient Chatsworth was because she could sit in her drawing room and be completely unaware of the fact that a thousand people were wandering around the rest of the house. It's precisely the reverse in this household. When the kids are at home - all four of them - I sit in my drawing room and I can hear a thousand people thundering around the house.

SILLY AND DAFT

Herself will be the end of me. On Sunday she set off to drive north leaving me sweating over a hot spade in the garden. As she drove away I saw she had left her handbag on the roof of the car. I waved. I jumped up and down flailing the air like a drunken semaphoric sailor. She continued to wave back. Only my stentorian command "stop" - it was so loud it probably halted three regiments of Turkish foot soldiers - as she was disappearing from sight finally slowed her down. Why hadn't she stopped when I waved and leapt about? "I thought you were being your usual silly, daft self", she said.

DRAGON SLAYS ST GEORGE

I decided to amuse myself with a slight public humiliation of that woman to whom, alas, I am bound by ties of marriage. The missus is a tourist guide, and when I espied her outside St. John's College, explaining in her vivid manner the meaning of the heraldic beasts emblazoned upon that college's gateway to a group from the north of England, I strolled alongside and declaimed: "Rubbish, woman. Twaddle. Get your facts right". Without pause or change of tone the crone flung out a gesturing hand and cried for all to hear: "And there, 'midst all this beauty, is one of Cambridge's less attractive sights, my husband", and she continued with her erudite discourse to the titterings and guffaws of her attentive guests. I slunk away to the Blue Pig, defeated. It was a case of the dragon slaying St George.

Seasons and Flannelled Fools

A LYRICAL WAX

Just returned from a very long meander and I have this irresistable urge to wax. Lyrical, that is. Exult even. For once again I have proved to myself that we live in the smashingest country in the world and if that's not worth shouting about I know not what is.

You see, I was obliged to make a swift dash up to Lancashire last week and on my way home again I treated myself to the aforementioned meander. A pox upon motorways, said I and I set off for the lanes and byways of youthful memory. Across, then, into creamy Cheshire, all white-painted railings, lush meadows and every cow looking as though she had stepped straight out of an advertisement for Ovaltine, through the Peover (pronounced Peever, thank you) villages and past the Bells of Peover, a lovely old pub wherein the missus and I have oft-times supped; onwards into Derbyshire, dark and dankly beautiful and a quick wander on to my native moors. Only that day I had read a letter from a splendid chap who pointed out that following the Russian nuclear disaster our lives now depend literally upon which way the wind blows and so could we stop worrying about health food fads. And with that in mind I fell upon Bakewell like a ravening horde and denuded that splendid town of black puddings, Bakewell puddings, Derbyshire oat cakes, tomato flavoured sausages. Nelson's famed pork pies and other fattening loot with a feeling of inner glee.

I was home in time to listen to my bees working in the orchard, and to stroll on down Fen Lane to watch the swallows dining on the wing over the insect-rich lode. Proud cock pheasants were cackling in the woods, mallard were wheeling overhead but otherwise there was a stillness over the land and I felt hugely chuffed. Hence the waxing and the exultation.

Next morning I was back down the fen with my new binoculars having a shufty at the wildlife when a couple of the village lads came cycling by. They were both wearing those strange earphone things which, apparently, play music straight into the old lugholes. They were expressionless, away in another world and I felt so sorry for them. For on that bright and shiny morning I could hear the cuckoo. And the song of larks. And the sweet chirruping of countless songbirds. No man ever created music like that and those lads were the poorer for not harking to it.

FLANELLED FOOLS

This is ridiculous! Here we are, nowt but a skip and a jump from Midsummer's Day, and I'm writing this with a fire crackling in the grate behind me, rain coming down outside like a frenzied waterfall and half a gale tousling the tops of the trees.

What roses we have are bedraggled and mournful, furious at having bothered to turn out in this foul weather. And yet - brother nettle stands firm and jolly and while cossetted seedlings cower their neighbouring weeds burst into quick and uncontrollable growth.

Funny old world.

But never mind the plants. They can fend for themselves. It's the cricketers who worry me. There they are, frozen up to the pavilion steps, trying to pretend they are enjoying themselves as they are lashed by winter's wild lament. It's a terrible time for 'em as I recall from my own cricketing past.

Whenever I feel pangs of regret for having packed up playing this most glorious of games I brush away my sorrow by recalling those endless hours of sheer torture playing with blue-numb hands the while praying that the slimy, slippery ball would land anywhere around the field except close to one's own soggy person. There can be few more terrifying moments in life - except for the eyeball to eyeball confrontation with the taxman - than to be standing under the leaden sky of a coldly wet evening with that dreadful ball droping down towards your outstretched hands which are suddenly ten frozen fish fingers. After particularly strong cheese for supper I still wake up in the middle of the night, all of a muck sweat, dreaming about such times.

But then there are sweet dreams also of shimmering summers in the field when the whole day can be idled away in sensuous cricketing pleasure.

Idled away? Why, certainly. My long-time friend George Fletcher of this parish - and one of the best known and liked milkmen in Cambridge - and I established what was without a sliver of doubt the idlest fielding partnership in East Anglia, if not the entire cricketing world.

It worked in this fashion: George and I, you see, share a natural capacity for continuous corporeal expansion, the result of which was, in our cricketing days, that we were somewhat girthful to put it mildly.

But we served loyally under a number of understanding captains who realised (they would have been as thick around the head as we were around the waist if they hadn't) that we were not built for sprinting around the outfield.

Thus game after splendid game saw George and yours truly occupying the positions of mid-on and mid-off and for those two or three non-cricketers reading this that meant that we were allowed to stand far enough away from the batsman not to be in any danger of being hit by the ball but close enough to be incapable of stopping it.

At the end of each over, instead of us crossing the wicket to take up our new positions as is the normal requirement, George and I would simply stay where we were having turned slowly round to face the opposite direction.

And since we rarely got ourselves involved in the nonsense of scoring runs which could have meant dashing about between the wickets we were able to spend our summers happily standing around contemplating the beer to come or sunning ourselves outside the pavilion while the other flannelled fools got on with winning the game.

Which now brings me to the bombastic bit. Those of you who watched the Australian film last week about the bodyline bowling sensation of the 1930s could not do what I have been doing ad nauseum ever since: and that is to boast as I can that my father played against Harold Larwood who knocked the Aussies about something 'orrible with his 100 mile an hour deliveries.

The great Harold and my old man were kids together in neighbouring pit villages and the young Harold put the fear of God into my dad's team just as he was to do later in that most famous of Test matches.

My father still recalls his games against Larwood. He speaks of them through gritted teeth.

"DEARLY BELOVED"

Dearly beloved brethren, let us begin this harvest Festival with a parable concerning an old man who is witnessed planting fruit trees on the edge of his beloved cricket field. A youngster inquires of the ancient: "But why do you perform this task in the fullness of your years when you will never see the trees in their maturity?" To which the old man, eyes atwinkle, replies in this manner: "Because, my son, had my father not done the same thing there would have been no sweet greengages for me to pick when I was a boy here". Now this parable is not an allegory but a true tale and the planting of the trees took place recently on the boundary of the cricket ground at Lode. The moral of the yarn will be unveiled in due course but meanwhile let us take as our first reading a line or two from Jeremiah chapter 8 verse 20: "The harvest is past, the summer is ended, and we are not saved". And, yea, let us take a further text from 1 King's , 19;12: "And after the fire a still small voice." Now, brethren, thou hast cottoned on. It's farmers we are talking about. Or rather, those few cowboys who ride roughshod over the eastern prairies, uprooting our hedges and trees and scorching the very earth itself. Yea, verily, they are a dastardly shower and their insensitivity will surely bring upon their heads the wrath of their neighbours. Now, my children, you will see the connection between the old man and his greengages and the greedy men who render our landscape sterile. The one thinks of the next generation with foresight and compassion. The latter do not give an ear of wet corn for the future. Here endeth the Lesson.

HAUNCH OF WINTER

How did you enjoy that chill which crept into the weather on Sunday? I thought it was smashing and very, very English for in my view this overheated summer has been a mite too continental. We have toasted our toes for too long this year before a foreign fire and on Sunday as I watched some of the lads from the Cambridge fire brigade playing cricket in our village I noticed we had returned to reality with wives huddling in the lee of the pavilion to keep warm, kids running about with faces pinched by the cold. That's the true English summer scene, methought as I downed a pint through chattering teeth.

The fact is that spring is for dancing children, summer is for a loveliness of ladies whilst autumn and winter should be the preserve of men. We Englishmen are improperly accoutred for the soft days and I admit to feeling undressed unless I am equipped with tie and coat. So roll on the days of hoary breath and tweeds, of skating and shooting, of evening books and crackling fires. I can sing happily in the haunch of winter.

OLD LUCK SPINNERS

Suddenly over that glorious, sunny, smoky weekend, those old luck spinners were out and about in their millions and anyone with a phobia about spiders was best kept indoors.

We first noticed them on the Saturday when we were over at Chippenham after partridge. Down by our straggling stream the hot air was constantly alive with floating luck spinners - money spiders, call 'em what you will - and they cast their trails of gossamer over the fields with massive abandon until the stubble was coated in tresses of sheer, shiny silk..

Tiny and harmless they scuttled about in our hair, slithered down our open shirts and gaily skated along our gun barrels through the long, hot day, safe, I suppose, in the knowledge that they are protected from harm by centuries of inbred human belief that ill-luck befalls he who kills a spider. You still hear folk hereabout saying: "If you wish to live and thrive, let a spider run alive" - though I can tell you that after half a century of kindess to money spiders I am still awaiting my reward, my recompense.

They were out again when we were at the Town Plate on the July Course at Newmarket on Sunday where many in the huge crowd spent much of their time brushing the insects away, an act of unforgiveable folly especially on a race-track where it is absolutely de rigeur to refrain from spitting in the eye of chance. I have seen grown men at Newmarket tremble with sudden rage when some thoughtless twerp removes a passing money spider.

And, on our way home, the cricket field in our village was entirely sheathed in their gossamer. The sun's reflection from the silver threads was blinding, eerie, but a rare and beautiful picture.

But where did all those spiders come from? I dunno. But of one thing I am now certain: the old belief that spiders only spin on dark days ("The subtle spider never spins, But on dark days, his slimy gins") was utterly disproved last weekend when they worked like wanton furies throughout the brightest of hot Autumnal days.

Mark you, not all spiders have been saved by our fear of bad luck for it was also firmly believed in the fens that spiders were certain cures for rheumatism and the ague and, indeed, other fevers. The favourite trick, apparently was to wear a spider in a container - often a nutshell - around the neck. Although, if you wanted to cure jaundice you simply caught the nearest decent sized house spider, rolled him up in a dollop of butter, and swallowed him!

Gossamer, when you think about it, just has to be at one and the same time the most useless and yet the most beautiful of all nature's gifts. You can do nowt with it but marvel at it and be thankful to have seen it.

There are differing legends as to its origins but I prefer to stick to the one which tells us that gossamer was the ravelling of the Virgin Mary's winding sheet which fell to earth when she ascended to heaven. Unbeatable, that one.

FINEST OF SEASONS

You will recall that with the dawn on Sunday came the second of this autumn's frosts and a cold, glittering sunshine. When we had returned from Ely the previous night some unknown friend had left a bag of huge mushrooms hanging on the back door knob and my mind dwelt upon them as I walked off down to the fen on that lovely Sabbath morn. The cold air tingled the ear tips and forced a smarter pace. At Cow Bridge a small covey of grey partridges lifted from farmer Butler's field, skimming the heap of sugar beet, first of the season. Beyond, further out in his field, another covey of partridges fanned out and ran away in a widening circle like a platoon of attacking infantry. The heron that's been hanging around for some days floated upwards from the bank of the lode and lolloped off down to lonelier waters. A mother swan hissed at me, Peter Singleton's guinea fowl cackled with derision, as usual, when they saw me while lapwings in their scores dappled the big potato field black and white as they rose and fell in cumbersome flight. Over the pheasant woods came the chime of eight from the clock atop Swaffham Prior House and, Dick Whittington-like, I turned again, this time for home. There, awaiting me I knew, was crisp bacon and fat, fen mushrooms with the texture of molten silk.

Simple I might be. Contented certainly.

Somebody wrote of "congenial autumn" being "the sabbath of the year" whilst Shelley said: "There is a harmony in autumn and a lustre in its sky". It is, in my view, the finest of the seasons. But why? Mainly, perhaps, because there is a certainty about it. Whilst spring is the harbinger of good things to come it carries no guarantee; summer is a feckless mistress - never did know one to make up its mind in fifty years. Winter, too, can be kind or harsh. But with autumn we know where we are. It is a winding down time and nothing can prevent the year coming to its end. It is the glorious season for tweeds, for puddens, for breathing cool, clear air, for putting away the gardening tools, for preparing to rest through the long, dark nights. It is a time for the re-reading of favourite books, for the planning of hearty feasts, for the splitting of logs. And, best of all for many of us, it is the time to clean up the gun and take once again to the woods, the dykes, the moors, the meres.

Autumn would also seem to be a mixture of custom and high tech for I hear of the bright lad who put his conkers in the microwave to harden 'em up.

Actually, I can't remember ever finding an efficient way of hardening conkers in the distant days of my youth. I seem to recall soaking them in vinegar before putting 'em into the fireside, blackleaded oven. And much importance was placed on the care with which the hole was drilled and the type of string used. We haven't got a microwave so is there another new answer to the old conker question? I'd like to know because I might earn a few bob from some of the blokes at the Oak before the conker season ends.

YELLOW AS WORN GUINEAS

It's Saturday morning. Out early in the still heat to find the first of the sweet peas in bloom. Roses, as palely yellow as worn guineas, cling to the pink brickwork of our old house. A cascade of honeysuckle pours over the orchard wall. We watch the Trooping on the television, a glass of English champagne (some call it cider) at our side and marvel at the monarch's calm. We lunch outside. And we potter in the garden. There are many busy bees and blackbirds who eye the raspberry canes with greedy anticipation. There is good beer in the Oak and much laughter. I'm beginning to like England.

THE GOOD TIMES

Looked around our cricket ground on Sunday afternoon while they were playing the Six-a-Side tournament and it came to me suddenly that I'm getting on a bit. Many of the sturdy trees around the ground were but saplings when we first came to the village. And some of the lads who were playing were not even a twinkle in their father's eye when we arrived. Dear old Alan Irons, with whom I have shared many a happy hour with bat, with gun and with pint during the past quarter century, was playing with his smashing new granddaughter. Alan, a grand-dad! "We are getting on a bit, my old son," I said. "Does it matter, boy," he replied? "We've had some good times and they can't take those away."

Whereupon we had another pint apiece.

FAITHFUL WADDLER

The only sounds are the unending, but never wearisome, coo-ooings of wood pigeons in distant trees and the very gentlest soughing of the softest summer breeze. It is seven of the morning on Sunday and neither tractor nor motor car breaks the natural silence. Raucous lawn mowers lie still abed and the stuttering explosion of weekend aircraft engines are not yet ripping the skies apart.

The ditch is bulging with brown bullrushes and a cloud of brown-spotted butterflies dance like a wisp of happy snipe. I walk alone until I meet the only other walking creatures in that huge landscape, our friendly village shopkeeper Mrs Rosemary Upton and her faithful, waddling companion, Monty, her hound. We are agreed immediately that this is the countryside at the peak of perfection - golden crops ready for harvest, utter peace, air as refreshing as champagne. It is, we say, the best time of the day and we agree that it is just as well that others prefer to slumber on otherwise the fen would be filled with noisome folk. We exchange courtesies and continue our walks in different directions around the village. Oh, what a beautiful morning! Oh, what a beautiful day!

ONE HIT - 79 RUNS

Yes, of course, I know perfectly well what's happening next week and I'm sure we're all going to have the most smashingest of times and, yes, I'm equally certain that it will snow and if you can't explain to the kiddleywinks how Father-you-know-Who is going to materialise out of the central heating system then hard luck. You shouldn't have done away with the chimley.

Meanwhile to cricket.

You see, I'm standing in the County Farmers Club in Cambridge the other evening as is my occasional wont or will engulfed by a mass of seasonal decorations and warmed by the first glass of decent port for a month or several when I fall into conversation of a general manner with Master David Papworth, a jovial sprite of a fellow who farms in that most charmingly-named corner of Cambridgeshire, October End at Mepal, near Ely.

Now when two old sportsmen fall into each other's chatter it matters not what the season may be; there is an inevitability that within seconds they will come to a 'natterin' about a mutual interest.

And so it was with Master David and your humble servant for we quickly discovered that in years past we had each played upon the same fenland wickets - some (not many) immaculate, some where cattle had but recently left behind signs of their quaint ability to transmogrify the grass they have just eaten and others where the roundness of the cricket ball was rendered purposeless by the scattering of small boulders and bunkers just in front of the batsmen.

Oh aagh, we agreed, we had indeed had some hairy old experiences here and there around th'old fens.

Whereupon Master Papworth began to smile. This was followed by a chortle which rapidly became a guffaw. And this is the tale he told me:

Seems there was a tightly played old game going on over at the Witcham ground near Ely some time back - I believe David's father was playing at the time but I may be wrong because his laughter is infectious and I was beginning to fall about somewhat at this stage of the telling - when the local baker driving a pony and trap decided to take a short cut on his way back to Sutton by clip-clopping over the corner of the cricket field.

A batsman skied the ball and it landed, unbeknown to the baker, in some cloths in the back of his cart. Before a fielder could reach him and unhearing of the shouts he cleared the cricket ground, put whip to tail and went off at a fine speed towards welcoming home.

The opposition side claimed it was a lost ball. No, ruled the umpire, everybody knew where that old ball was. It was in the back of that old cart. The fielders set off in frantic pursuit. God knows how far they ran but Master David assured me that by the time they hailed the baker to stop they had to throw the ball back to the ground in relays. And the batsmen, he said, with tears in clear fenny eyes, had run 79 runs by the time the ball was declared dead.

Blast, bor, I should've loved to have seen that, says I to him.

ANTEPODEAN REVENGE

Did your head hang in shame at the weekend humiliation of our country's cricketers by New Zealand? If so, pull yourself together and be of stout heart for English cricket is about to enter a new and glorious phase. Well that was the impression I got at the annual meeting of our village club up in the upstairs room of the Oak on Monday night.

You see, we've been promoted into the next division of the Cambs League and nothing can prevent us from climbing to the very top and since I no longer play for them I can see nothing to stop 'em.

Indeed, as the ale went down so our spirits and enthusiasm soared and come closing time I had difficulty restraining some of them from setting off there and then for the Antipodes in order to avenge our national disgrace.

The dozy cricket club re-elected me chairman again which clearly demonstrates their intellectual bankruptcy. It is, however, a position totally without responsibility, power, influence or authority for the cunning lads make all the important decisions before the meeting and then treat me with the sort of firm good humour normally reserved for the very young or the dodderer.

Nevertheless I'd give my old shut knife and a decent piece of string to be out with the flannelled fools again this summer.

NOT OUT!

Before I take to the field to umpire on Sunday at that exciting cricketing extravaganza, the Swaffham Bulbeck Six-a-Side Tournament, I will cleanse myself with confession. Once, when I was umpiring, the bowler appealed after rapping the batsman's pad in front of the wicket and I gave a firm "not out". Hailing from Bottisham, he naturally objected to my decision, and asked me to oblige him with an explanation. Firstly, said I, the ball was moving to leg, secondly it was rising above the height of the bails and thirdly the batsman was my son and if he wanted to get him out he had better knock his stumps down and even then I might shout "no ball". The bowler was nonplussed but he never argued again. I mention the shameful episode in order to assure Sunday's bowlers that Simon is not playing for the Swaffhams and I will be my usual unbiased self. Bowl with confidence.

CORKED

Flaming June! As I write there is the sound of crackling and spitting as the logs in the old fireplace burn with some merriment. And I'm still friz up to the elbows. Outside all is damp and decay and Sebastian Herbert, our cat, cowers under a soggy lilac tree, lacklustre, soaked and about as happy as a frog with a sore throat. Furthermore, my horse came 14th in the Derby, the bottle of claret I opened for dinner was corked and our asparagus appears to have gone on strike.

Flaming June!

One of the chief joys of my life at this time of the year is in being able to step out of the back door, stroll four yards, take my ancient shut knife from my pocket and cut three pounds or so of the aforementioned asparagus. That joy, alas, is currently being denied me because the flaming June weather has turned my crop of that queen of vegetables into a mood of total recalcitrance. So much so that when each purple tip appears, it simply takes a quick sniff, snorts with chill derision, and goes back to bed again. For three pounds read ten sticks.

CUSHCOW LADIES

When all around is change and decay, uncertainty and illusion, then 'tis a blessed comfort to be reminded of one of life's absolute doctrines and this is precisely what happened to me whilst bent double in the garden the other afternoon just before the sciatica felled me.

For there among the weeds crawling and tumbling over themselves in their frenzy to enjoy at last the spring sunshine were ladybirds in their hundreds; a scene of great and refreshing delight. But what, pray, I hear you asking, is this unchallengable dogma, this steadfast belief to which I refer? Well, it is the countryman's secure knowledge of the all-round goodness of the ladybird and his traditional abhorrence at the prospect of any ill befalling these lovely insects. An utterly benign little bug, she neither bites nor stings, bringing enchantment into the world of the wondering child and delight to the gardener. And she is so well-named, this exquisite creature, more gorgeously caparisoned than any duchess's fancy jewels, for she is named after Our Lady because of the marvellous service she renders mankind by feasting voraciously upon the dreaded greenfly. Ladybird, ladyfly, ladycow - these are her names (though in Yorkshire you will hear her called cushcow lady).

She also inspires one of the saddest yet most oft-repeated of nursery rhymes and, though these days one risks accusation of being a sexist, racist or alarmist by quoting any innocent piece of doggerel, I would like to put before you an unusual version of the ladybird rhyme:

"Ladycow, ladycow, fly thy way home / Thy house is on fire, thy children all gone / All but one that ligs under a stone / Ply thee home, ladycow, ere it be gone".

How many millions of ladybirds have crawled along how many millions of podgy little fingers over the centuries whilst children have chanted that rhyme, I wonder? Welcome back, ladycow.

OH- TO BE IN ENGLAND....

Phone rang at the weekend. My number two daughter Rachel, a much-travelled young lady, is on the other end. She's holidaying in southern Spain with her constant companion Dick Bradford from the next village. No, she said, the weather over there was behaving very badly. No, she said, they had not much enjoyed their week in north Africa mainly because of the bad local food, and bad local manners and the endless local flies. How was England? Well, says I, it's hot, but there's a cooling breeze. The sky is eggshell blue and cloudless. The budleia is a mass of flittering butterflies. Your ma's reading in the orchard where the bees hum loud. I've just picked six vegetables for lunch. There's cricket on the rec and the Black Horse is open all afternoon. England, says I, is in good order. Rachel mutters a word which I can only imagine she picked up during her visit to the casbah for it is unfamiliar to me. Serves you right, says I. Oh, says I, oh, you should be in England now that summer's finally arrived.

Actually, I was a bit late getting to the cricket match because after lunch herself and I both re-adjourned to the orchard with the Sunday papers and the deckchairs. I chose the deep shade whilst herself sunbathed for the first time this year. As my eyelids lowered in preparation for the inevitable kip I spotted a piece in The Observer which was balm to the soul, honey to the heart. In effect the story said that new research shows that people who enjoy a quiet snooze after Sunday lunch may be doing themselves a bit of good. For Greek doctors have found that even a 30-minute siesta (do Greeks have siestas? Isn't there a Greek word for this most marvellous portion of one's day?) could help to reduce the risk of heart attack by up to thirty percent.

At this point I was so overwhelmed by the realisation that, because I have enjoyed a siesta every day over the years, I am now due to live forever, I dived into deep oblivion, with the sunlight slipping through the leaves to dapple my occasional, self-satisfied dream.

PLEASURES COME TRIPPING QUICKLY

Hours later, this time sitting under a conker tree with Percy Blinco and his missus, we watched our village lads thrashing a visiting team from London Town. The other lot, a very pleasant crowd I should add, were from the Grosvenor House Hotel in Park Lane and I fear their fitness had become somewhat impaired by an obvious over-consumption of the splendid gastronomic delicacies which the chefs at the great hotel are able to offer. Any way, our lads hit 'em all round the ground and out of it and nearly as much time was spent looking for lost balls as fetching pitchers of ale from the Black Horse.

Back home I can smell the strawberry jam as it bubbles away in a huge pan in the kitchen. Raspberry jam cools in a dozen big jars. On the table the redcurrant jelly oozes through the muslin, clear as new claret. Just about every room in the house is awash with the gentle scent of sweet peas. Outside the elderberries are forming, the conker tree is heavily laden already promising a bumper crop, the carrots are the length of a slim little finger, baby broad beans at their tastiest. This, my friends is cornucopia time, the time of plenty. Further, there's fresh bread and crumbly Lancashire cheese in the pantry and Bob Scrutton's beer at The Oak is in fine fettle, so, to tell the truth, I don't care a fig if it rains or freezes. And come to think of it, we're going to have a lot of figs this year as well. Millions I may lack but my pleasures come tripping quickly. Tally-ho, whoopee....

RAMADIN AND WEEKS

Now a lot of clever things have been said about cricket over the years but I picked out a new beauty from a recent lecture given by Bernard Williams, Provost of King's and former Knightbridge Professor of Philosophy at Cambridge. He was referring to the "overwhelming Englishness" of some obscure book (the very title baffled my bird brain) but he used the simile of a cricket match which, he said "has the very sophisticated feature that one can only appreciate the significant detail of the monotony that lies before one at a given time because one understands remote and hypothetical moments of excitement which might grow from it." Bernard Williams' fluency in the use of our language fills me with a dreadful envy and no wonder they call him the cleverest man in England. But I'll let you into another small secret: I've known him long enough to bet you a florin to a pinch of snuff that he scarcely recognises one end of a cricket racquet from the other.

Sorry about the name-dropping but I bumped into Edward Miller, newly retired Master of Fitzwilliam College who was delighted with both cricket and sweltering sun at Fenners last week. He recalled that memorable game in 1950 when Cambridge were massacred by the West Indians whose 703 for 3 is likely to stand as the highest ever score against the Varsity. Mr Miller entertained bowler Ramadin and batsman Weeks to dinner in his college. Everton Weeks hobbled in complaining that the cold had given him chilblains. He would be obliged, he told Mr Miller, to play off his back foot the following day. He hobbled onto the ground. And scored 304 not out.

SKATES AND MAD HARES

As March comes roaring in like a polar bear and our spirits continue to sink with the temperature kindly allow me to pass on a snippet of information which is guaranteed to bring a small smirk to the lips, a twinkle to the eyes and, from those who are my close friends, a great big belly laugh: I've got gout again...

Funny old month, March. The Saxons knew it as Hreth-monath (rough month) or Hlyd-monath (boisterous month) and the farmers have always reckoned that a bushel of March dust is worth a king's ransom. This year, however, I suspect the farmers will be pleased with a touch of damp in the ground for February was noticeably reluctant to fill her dykes. Altogether this remarkable cold spell has been a desperate blow to the farmers and winter sown crops have suffered badly. There'll be many who will be redrilling wheat and barley fields this spring. And that old oil seed rape is looking distinctly sickly. Terrible times when you start feeling really sorry for the farmers.

And though we are now into March good and proper still the skating goes on and, frankly, were it not for the current attack of the dreaded salmon and trout, I would this very Monday morning be having a gentle whizz round over at Earith.

My old chum Derek Tunnicliffe, that most excellent Cambridge solicitor, was out there on his skates on Sunday and over a pint in the Oak later he was telling me that the last time he managed a March skate in the fens was on March 4, 1963, a glorious day as he recalls, for after skating he went home and was able to sit outside in the sunshine wearing indoor clothes. It's his recollection, and mine too, that there has been no bearing ice since then in March until this peculiar year of 1986 and we both agreed that we twain will probably never have the chance of a March skate again, what with anno domini and all that.

Still, one of the chief pleasures of March will soon be upon us again. I refer to the charming activities of the Mad March Hares who will shortly be dancing and prancing and boxing their way around the fields. Jack Hare loves to put on his wild display of standing on hind legs and boxing away with his opponent during the rutting season in order to impress the watching ladies. And 'tis as well, methinks, that humans are not similarly afflicted for I know some blokes up at the Oak who would be boxing each other 24 hours a day, 352 days a year.

THE FATEFUL CLICK

Son Simon, who wields a nifty willow occasionally, was bowled first ball in his first game of cricket on Saturday and afterwards we discussed that special, stomach-churning sensation all cricketers feel when they hear the fateful click of ball on wicket. I've felt it more than most, I fear, and there are only two other sounds which produce the same effect: the announcement of a stewards' inquiry after you think you've backed the winner and the cry of "Time, Gentlemen, please" as you queue to buy your first pint.

"AH! YOU SHOULD HAVE SEEN.........."

A double sadness this week. The last of the sweet peas have been cut and the daily delight of harvesting those humble, fragrant flowers which brighten and perfume the dullest of days is over for another year. And, through it drives a stiletto through my heart to confess it, I finally threw away my last pair of cricket boots on Sunday during a huge house clear-out. We all know when our cricketing days are finished but by hanging old boots up in a safe place there remains the optimist's hopeless dream of one last, magnificent innings; a slashing, cutting, driving, clouting innings which will be writ large in the verbal history books of the game so that down the years old men will murmur over their beer to young cricketers: "Ah, but you should have been there for Jeacock's last game ...."